GW00671635

Athletic CEOs

Athletic CEOs

Leadership in Turbulent Times

**STANISLAV SHEKSHNIA, VERONIKA ZAGIEVA
AND ALEXEY ULANOVSKY**

ANTHEM PRESS

Anthem Press
An imprint of Wimbledon Publishing Company
www.anthempress.com

This edition first published in UK and USA 2018
by ANTHEM PRESS
75–76 Blackfriars Road, London SE1 8HA, UK
or PO Box 9779, London SW19 7ZG, UK
and
244 Madison Ave #116, New York, NY 10016, USA

British Library Cataloguing-in-Publication Data
A catalogue record for this book is available from the British Library.

ISBN-13: 978-1-78308-759-4 (Hbk)
ISBN-10: 1-78308-759-5 (Hbk)

This title is also available as an e-book.

Contents

Illustrations

Figures

Tables

Introduction

Athletic CEOs: Leadership in Turbulent Times is a book about high-performing transformational leaders operating in turbulent environments. These CEOs do not lead by the book: they may not praise their subordinates, provide positive feedback or regularly celebrate small wins. Yet they have created formidable enterprises that deliver sustainable growth, have elevated their companies' employees to new levels, have set new standards for their industries and have advanced their regions. Most remarkably, in spite of their prominence, these leaders continue to reinvent themselves. The focus of this book is not on what effective leadership should look like but on how it looks like in a specific context. It follows an approach advocated by Jeffrey Pfeffer in his recent book *Leadership BS*: 'If we want to change the world of work and leadership conduct in many workplaces, we need to act on what we know rather than what we wish and hope for.'[1]

In 2007, when Herman Gref, ex-minister of economic development and trade of the Russian Federation, became CEO of Sberbank, the largest and arguably the most inefficient bank in the country, no one believed that the former bureaucrat, who had never worked in business, could transform this cumbersome organization that had become a byword for poor customer service and inefficiency. Almost ten years later, even outright sceptics admit that

---

[1] J. Pfeffer, *Leadership BS: Fixing Workplaces and Careers One Truth at a Time* (New York: HarperBusiness, 2015).

1

Sberbank has risen from the half-dead. Client managers have begun to smile, queues have disappeared and 30 per cent of customers access all the bank's services via their smartphones or computers without ever setting foot in a branch. Financial results have followed the clients: during Gref's tenure, Sberbank's assets have increased more than fivefold, and operating income has grown by over 20 per cent a year. In the year 2016/17 alone, Sberbank's capitalization grew from US$30 billion to US$62 billion dollars.

The scale of the 300,000-strong organization's transformation is breathtaking. Gref and his team have created a world-class IT platform, launched shared-service centres and built Sberbank Corporate University to educate employees about cutting-edge management practices. Sberbank has become the trendsetter for the whole country's banking industry: it was the first in Russia to implement a lean production approach, to introduce agile innovation methods and to address the blockchain revolution. All of this was achieved against the backdrop of a global financial crisis and two local recessions.

If Sberbank is the "circulatory system" (according to its annual report) of the Russian economy, then Aeroflot is its wings. Like Sberbank, Aeroflot, one of the oldest carriers in the world, was famous for its poor service and consequent customer drain. When new CEO Vitaly Saveliev joined the company in April 2009, Aeroflot had only just enough money to continue operating for two more weeks. Experts advised him to change the brand, which was indelibly associated with communism, and to solve the problems of constant delays and bad flight experiences.

Seven years later, Aeroflot was ranked the world's most powerful airline brand. The company was consistently winning international awards for its service quality and positive international press reviews. Of all European airlines, it had the highest customer loyalty index (with a 'Net Promoter Score' of 72 per cent). Passenger turnover had risen from 11 million a year to 43 million, while revenues had grown from US$3.3 billion to US$7.4 billion. With an average age of 4.2 years, Aeroflot also had one of the youngest fleets in the world.

Success allowed Aeroflot to be more active in lobbying for initiatives affecting the whole aviation industry, such as permission for Russian airlines to hire foreign pilots, stricter penalties for in-flight brawls and ratification of non-refundable tariffs. In exchange, Aeroflot had to carry out social obligations, such as launching 'flat tariffs' aimed at improving accessibility to the strategically important regions of Russia, even if they were not profitable for the company.

When in 1989 Eugene Kaspersky detected one of the first computer viruses (Cascade) on his desktop computer and subsequently cured it, he did not realize that this would be the first step in generating hundreds of millions of dollars in revenue for his future company and an important milestone in the history of the emergent cybersecurity industry. Today, the name 'Kaspersky' is known to every computer user as one of the leading endpoint security vendors, protecting more than 400 million users and 270,000 corporate clients in 200 countries.

Established in 1997, Kaspersky Lab targeted the global market from day one, building a partnership network all over the world. The quality of its products and the speed of its updates became the main selling points and enabled the company to position itself as a provider of premium products. Kaspersky Lab has never lost its technological superiority. In 2015, Kaspersky Lab products participated in 94 independent tests and reviews and were awarded 60 first places and 77 top-three rankings. Kaspersky Lab employs a Global Research and Analysis Team (GReAT), an elite group of leading security experts who operate all over the world and provide top-notch anti-threat intelligence and research. In recent years, this team has discovered and disarmed many of the world's most sophisticated cyberespionage and cybersabotage threats, such as Flame, Gauss and Red October, preventing potential losses of hundreds of millions of dollars. It assists national governments and international security bodies in cyberthreat investigations, holds regular training courses for Interpol and Europol officers and the police forces of many countries and hosts the Kaspersky Lab Security Analyst Summit for the best IT security experts from all over the world.

In his ten years as the CEO of the Russian oil major Gazprom Neft, Alexander Dyukov transformed the company from an industry underdog to the most dynamic oil company in the country. Its reserves grew from 720 million tons to 1.5 billion tons, annual hydrocarbons production rose from 46 to almost 86 million tons in oil equivalent and refining increased from 24 to 42 million tons. Gazprom Neft's revenue grew from US$20 billion (548 billion roubles) to more than US$23 billion (1,545 billion roubles) during Dyukov's reign – all in spite of a significant fall in the price of oil.

Under Dyukov's leadership Gazprom Neft reversed the trend of declining production by broadening its portfolio of greenfield projects and increasing the efficiency of its brownfield assets – and became the industry leader in extracting difficult-to-access oil, drilling horizontally and developing innovative digital or smart fields. The company also worked intensively on its image for end consumers. It developed a network of gas stations, conducted rebranding and introduced loyalty programmes which resulted in a doubling of its average daily sales volumes per station, becoming one of the market leaders in Russia. In a market dominated by sluggish state-owned oil companies, Gazprom Neft stands apart thanks to its proactive approach. In 2013 Gazprom Neft became the first company to produce oil from the Russian Arctic shelf, requiring the construction of an innovative offshore, ice-resistant stationary platform. The company has also been very active in developing international markets. It has embarked on joint ventures in Venezuela and Iraq, and acquired assets in Serbia and Italy.

This book offers a model of leadership which delivers superior results in a specific context, that is, one of fast obsolescence, high turbulence, intense government interference, mediocre levels of human capital development and traditionally high levels of managerial control. We call it athletic leadership (AL), since we find strong parallels between our protagonists' attitudes and behaviours and those of top sportspeople. Our athletic leaders all share a formative experience of practicing competitive sports in their youth, facing early adversity as leaders of important projects and changing companies and industries along the way. They possess two traits that define their leadership personality: mental toughness and adaptability. Toughness leads to passionate, focused and merciless pursuit of ambitious goals such as 'creating a digital company to compete with the Googles and Amazons'[2] (Gref)

[2] Herman Gref's speech, *Sberbank' Annual Shareholders Meeting*, 26 May 2017.

or 'saving the world'[3] (Kaspersky). Adaptability allows for rapid knowledge reinvigoration and the constant updating of mental models and business paradigms. Athletic CEOs use some specific iterative behavioural and mental strategies to conduct their jobs, which we call the 'meta-practices' of athletic leadership. They deliver superior operational and financial results (leadership outputs) as well as transform their followers, companies, industries and communities (leadership outcomes).

We started our research and developed our model by looking at leaders in Russia, but we found athletic CEOs elsewhere in industries with similar contexts – like oil and gas, banking, pharmaceuticals, metals, telecoms or the Internet – and in some emerging markets – like China, Brazil or Turkey. The model of athletic leadership has proven itself globally.

This book has been written for people who are interested in the subject of leadership in business: executives, middle managers, professionals, MBAs and undergraduate students, coaches, consultants, leadership development specialists, educators and scholars. We believe that it also offers some interesting ideas and practical insights for people from other areas of life such as politics, government and education.

We tried to write this book in a reader-friendly way, keeping in mind business practitioners as our main target audience. We left the description of our research methodology and process out of the main body and put it into a separate appendix instead. We list literature for further reading at the end of chapters.

There are different ways to read this book. 'Traditional' readers may go through all the chapters in order and finish with the conclusion. 'Busy' readers may limit their efforts to the first three chapters, which explain the model of athletic leadership and describe each of its elements, along with Chapter 9, which offers lessons to different categories of leaders and the general public. 'Story lovers' may start by reading Chapters 4 to 8, which are devoted to the cases of four athletic CEOs in Russia and three in Brazil, China and the United States and then progress to the more conceptual Chapters 1 to 3 and 9.

---

[3] D. Sacco, 'Eugene Kaspersky: Our Mission Is to Save the World', *PCR*, 18 March 2014.

We developed the model of athletic leadership by studying the biographies, experiences, narratives, actions, thoughts and emotions of real leaders operating in specific contexts. Over the last ten years we had the privilege to interview, work with and observe in action four CEOs – Alexander Dyukov, Herman Gref, Eugene Kaspersky and Vitaly Saveliev – and to speak with their followers, customers, partners and superiors as well as to study their company materials, premises and so on. We are deeply indebted to the four main 'characters' of this book and their organizations – and we would like to thank them for their willingness to talk and to share their thoughts. Without their contributions, this book would not have been possible. We also built on case studies of other leaders whom we got to know through our research and consulting work or through the work of other researchers: Oleg Bagrin, president of NLMK, a leading Russian steel producer; Sergey Frank, CEO of Sovkomflot, a Russian sea shipping company; Sergey Galitsky, founder and CEO of Magnit, the largest Russian retailer; Oleg Tinkov, founder and CEO of Tinkoff bank; Jeff Bezos, founder and CEO of Amazon; Roger Agnelli, ex-CEO of Vale; and Dong Mingzhu, CEO and later chair of Gree Electric. We have learned something valuable from each of their stories and we gratefully recognize their contribution to this book.

In addition, we had the privilege of speaking to some former top athletes: Viacheslav Fetisov, a many-time Olympic and World champion and captain of the famous Red Machine USSR ice-hockey team in the 1980s; Boris Lagutin, three times the Olympic boxing champion; Vladimir Muntyan, Cup of Cups and Super-Cup winner, many-time champion of the USSR and formerly the best footballer in the USSR; Viktor Rybakov, three-times the European Champion in boxing; and Helmut Wieser, currently CEO of AMAG Austria Metall and a world-class penthatlon athlete in 1970-1980s. These conversations provided unique insights into the minds and practices of top athletes and helped us formulate working hypotheses about athletic leadership. We highly appreciate the time, openness, reflectiveness, sense of humour and humbleness of our star interviewees.

We would like to acknowledge all the scholars who influenced the thinking on leadership that is presented in this book, but we would especially like to thank our teachers, who opened up the field of leadership and business studies to us and supported our early work: Professors Manfred Kets de Vries, Daniel McCarthy, Sheila Puffer.

We also would like to thank the institutional supporters of this project, particularly INSEAD's Emerging Markets Institute, and its academic director, Paddy Padmanabhan, and Ward Howell Talent Equity Institute for encouraging and financing our research. Finally, we would be remiss if we did not express our gratitude to Elin Williams for her unfaltering enthusiasm in editing the manuscript. Special thanks to Alexandra Matveeva from Ward Howell Talent Equity Institute for her invaluable help with data collection and analysis.

Many colleagues from academia have given us feedback and advice after reading the manuscript or parts of it and hearing our models. We would like to thank Professors Alena Ledeneva, Manfred Kets de Vries, Subi Rangan, Tim Rowley and Valery Yakubovich. We are very grateful to our clients, partners and friends from the business world who helped us develop the concepts presented in this book by listening, sharing and providing critique: George Abdushelishvili, Kirill Androsov, Gregory Fedorishin, Valery Katkalo, Pavel Kiryukhantsev, Kirill Kravchenko, Ekaterina Matskevich, Kirill Matveev, Dmitry Vasilkov, Oleg Polyakov, Ekaterina Ryasentseva, Sergey Sirotenko, Oleg Smirnov, Vitaly Vassiliev, Sergey Vorobiev.

The literature on leadership is enormous. By writing this book we wanted to make a small contribution to it by pointing in a new direction: highlighting leaders who are not perfect by the established standards of leadership but who achieve indisputably great results. We hope that this book brings us one step closer to a more balanced and nuanced picture of leadership and at the same time creates some inspiration for good leadership in tough times. It shows that, although athletic leadership is not for everyone or for every context, we can all learn from it. Athletic leaders teach us always to aim higher, never to stop developing and sometimes to adopt productive leadership practices that are not found in conventional textbooks.

1

Athletic Leadership Explained

Overpower. Overtake. Overcome.

— Serena Williams

My mother thinks I am the best. And I was raised to always believe what my mother tells me.

— Diego Maradona

Why *Athletic* Leadership?

Viacheslav Fetisov played his first professional hockey game at the age of 17 and his last at the age of 40. In his 22 seasons on ice, he had a distinguished career in both the leading hockey leagues of the time: the North American NHL and the USSR Top League. He won two Olympic gold medals and seven more at the World Championships as well as the regular season title of the NHL, the Stanley Cup and the Canada Cup. He was captain of the famous 'Red Machine', the USSR ice hockey team of the 1980s and leader of arguably the most powerful and creative quintet in ice hockey's history: Larionov-Krutov-Makarov-Fetisov-Kasatonov. Fetisov explained to us what distinguishes athletes and teams that consistently win at the highest level: 'If the next minute after listening to your national anthem and stepping down from the top of the podium you don't start thinking about how to beat your competitors again, you are finished as a champion.'[1] His words resonate with

---

[1] In interview with authors.

those of Saveliev, CEO of Aeroflot: 'I am not interested in celebrating old victories; I want to win new ones.'[2] The metaphor of 'athletic leadership' emerged at an early stage of our research. We noticed that all the leaders in our study shared an exceptional desire to win and to improve their performance – just like top-level athletes.

This observation made us look into the research on world-class athletes and led us to interview some of them. Our deep dive into the world of top sport yielded a number of interesting discoveries that reinforced the initial hypothesis about similarities between the leaders we studied and top-performing athletes.

Following the logic of Albert Bandura's triadic concept of human agency, we may look at athlete performance through three lenses: the athlete's behaviour, his or her personality and environmental events.[3] These factors interacting and influencing each other bi-directionally define performance. Performance is thus a function of three variables. First, what elite athletes do: how they train, compete and recover. Second, who they are: what cognitive, emotional, and personal abilities and traits they possess. Third, what kind of environment they train and compete in: external conditions that contribute to their performance (see Figure 1.1).

Environment

Athletes and researchers who study them speak about 'extreme pressure', 'ambiguity', 'uncertainty', 'permanent pressure' and 'intensifying competition' as intrinsic characteristics of the wider environment in which they have to compete. At the same time, athletes are the 'centres of gravity', the 'focus' and the 'focal points' of the narrower environments defined by the coaches, personal trainers, psychologists, dieticians, masseurs and other support staff who help them train, compete and recover. This is similar to business leaders who run companies that operate in turbulent, ever-changing, often hostile and always uncertain

[2] In interview with authors.
[3] A. Bandura, *Social Foundations of Thought and Action: A Social Cognitive Theory* (Englewood Cliffs, NJ: Prentice-Hall, 1986).

Figure 1.1 Model of Top Performance in Sports.

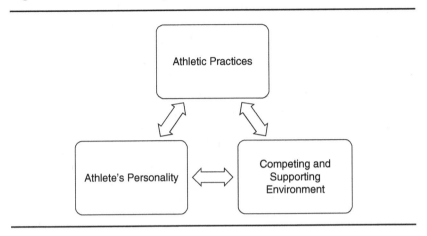

environments yet enjoy the full attention of numerous deputies, aides and assistants who surround them in the organization.

Practices

Three types of activities are essential for consistently winning at the top level in sports – training, competition and recreation. When training, top athletes put in extremely long hours and engage in a deliberate practice described by psychologist Anders Ericsson as 'requiring substantial mental and physical effort', 'targeting specific skills', 'eliminating weaknesses', 'never stopping to develop' and 'receiving clear feedback'.[4] Helmut Wieser, a former international pentathlon athlete, explained to us the difference between the legendary many-time Olympic and world champion Pavel Lednev and the rest: 'We would train with him all day, then we would go to bed and Lednev would go swimming.'[5] When competing, top athletes focus on winning, concentrate mentally and physically on the task, overcome pain and transcend the 'I can't.' Wieser continues, 'Once I ended up next to Lednev at the shooting range. He completely withdrew himself from the world,

---

[4] J. Starkes and K. A. Ericsson (eds), *Expert Performance in Sport: Recent Advances in Research on Sport Expertise* (Champaign, IL: Human Kinetics, 2003).

[5] In interview with authors.

concentrating on the target. He got 990 out of 1,000 points. I looked at him, his results, got nervous and screwed up my round.'[6] Recreation is based on letting go of physical pain and fatigue and incorporating new lessons into the personal knowledge database.

Although doing a very different type of a job, in which training, performance and recreation are often blended in a continuous set of activities, the business leaders we studied force themselves and their organizations to work at the edge of their physical, mental and intellectual capabilities, press hard to eliminate their weaknesses and learn both from victories and losses.

Personality

In discussing the mentality and personality of world-class athletes, sports commentators frequently describe them as 'tough', emphasizing their total focus on the task and uncompromising competition, tolerance for interference and pitilessness towards themselves.

Academics studying top athletes use the term 'mental toughness' to describe the key element of the top performers' personality.[7] Mental toughness is defined as a collection of inherent values, attitudes and emotions that help the athlete deliver sustainable high performance despite varying, challenging and unfavourable circumstances. Among the characteristics related to mental toughness are loving the pressure of competition, enjoying the bits of training that hurt, adapting to changes or threats and making the right decisions to secure optimal performance under extreme pressure and uncertainty. In her recent book, psychologist Angela Duckworth uses the term 'grit' to describe passion and perseverance towards long-term goals.[8] The leaders in our study

[6] In interview with authors.

[7] T. Coulter, C. J. Mallett and D. F. Gucciardi, 'Understanding Mental Toughness in Australian Soccer: Perceptions of Players, Parents, and Coaches', *Journal of Sports Sciences* 28 (2010): 699–716; D. F. Gucciardi and S. Gordon (eds), *Mental Toughness in Sport: Developments in Theory and Research* (Abingdon, Oxon: Routledge, 2011).

[8] A. Duckworth, *Grit: Why Passion and Resilience Are the Secrets to Success* (London: Vermilion, 2016).

possess similar personalities, which largely define their style of leadership. It is no accident that the word their subordinates most often use to describe their bosses is 'tough'.

Model of Athletic Leadership

Sport metaphors are nothing new in the leadership and business literature and are most often used as inspirational analogies. We use them because we see some profound similarities between top-performing athletes and effective CEOs operating in turbulent and highly regulated contexts. The term 'athletic' captures the essence of the latter's leadership – far reaching, competitive, determined and at times merciless. It shows strengths and potential as well as costs and a darker side. The metaphor also highlights similarities between the personality traits and practices of athletes and those of athletic leaders. At the same time this metaphor is not universal and has a limited applicability to a specific type of leadership, which emerged in a particular context and forms the subject of this book.

The similarities should not undermine significant differences between the performances of athletic CEOs and top athletes. Apart from the activities of heads of state, the complexity of CEOs work can hardly be compared to any other human activity. Our protagonists manage tens and even hundreds of thousands of employees, invest tens of billions of dollars and interact with presidents, ministers, global CEOs and international investment bankers. They have to deal with hundreds of variables on a daily basis. Their decisions and actions directly impact millions of people and indirectly affect hundreds of millions. Their organizational legacy will last for decades. To describe the essential elements of the athletic leadership, we have developed a nine-factor model, which is presented in Figure 1.2.

Formative Experience

A number of similar events happened in our athletic leaders' early lives, leaving a distinctive mark on their leadership.

All four of the main protagonists of this book had some exposure to *competitive sports* in their youth. Dyukov, Saveliev

Figure 1.2   Athletic Leadership Model.

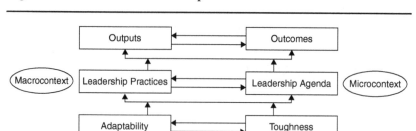

and Gref were respectively – fencing, boxing and high jump – champions in their junior years. Kaspersky sailed in his native town of Dolgoprudny. Similarly, Sergey Galitsky and Sergey Frank played football, while Oleg Bagrin has been a devoted rock climber for many years and Oleg Tinkov was a high-level amateur cyclist who still dreams of winning the Tour de France. We believe that athletic toughness and adaptability have some of their roots in these youthful activities.

These future athletic leaders occupied *leadership positions early in their lives* – when most of their contemporaries still had entry-level jobs. Saveliev ran a huge organization at the age of 28. At the same age, Gref became head of a property management fund in a town near St Petersburg, and Dyukov was appointed CFO of St Petersburg's oil terminal (and would become the CEO the following year). Kaspersky headed a group of software designers at the age of 26 and started his own business at the age of 31. Early exposure to leadership made these men comfortable running organizations and contributed to their self-confidence and winning mentality.

It is important to underline that the first leadership experiences of our future 'athletes' were not easy. We have already used this word many times, but when our protagonists speak about their early positions of responsibility, they all call them 'tough'. Saveliev ended up in a hospital bed. Dyukov had to negotiate with aggressive trade unions and semi-criminal vendors. Gref worked at the St Petersburg Property Committee in the 1990s, when the city was infamously known as 'Russia's criminal capital' – and some of his close associates were assassinated. Kaspersky had to lead a group of programmers without any seed capital in a country preoccupied with survival. These difficult leadership experiences gave our protagonists an advantage, making them strong but also somewhat rough-edged and assertive.

Most of the athletic leaders we came across – and all the protagonists of the book – are *industry outsiders*. They did not study to become bankers, oilmen, airline executives or anti-virus developers. Nor did they work their way up in one organization or industry. Even an entrepreneur like Kaspersky worked for two research institutes before starting his own business. Dyukov came to Gazprom Neft from a chemical company, Saveliev to Aeroflot from telecoms (via a government ministry) and Gref was himself a minister – who had never worked for a business before Sberbank. Exposure to different industries and organizations contributed to these leaders' adaptability and increased their ability to bring about organizational change.

Mental Toughness

Like top athletes, athletic leaders thrive in competition, push themselves and their organizations to the edge, and stay focused on the goal regardless of the external distractions.

Mental toughness creates a very stable base for athletic leadership, making it focused on winning, concentrated on results, robust and stress-proof. At the same time athletic leaders demonstrate high levels of flexibility in goal setting, strategizing and organizing execution. They exhibit *mental adaptability*, which is the skill of absorbing new information, updating mental models, and adjusting goals and ways to achieve them under changing circumstances. This tension between toughness and adaptability forms the mental foundation of athletic leadership.

Mental toughness can be broken down into five distinct – albeit related – components.

Super-sized Ambition

Just as Olympic and world champions are confident about their abilities to perform and succeed at that level, an athletic leader is sure about his capacity to bring an organization to the highest level of performance regardless of external circumstances. When Gref became Sberbank's CEO, he was not only a novice banker but also a novice CEO, yet he was confident that Sberbank would become a world-class organization and made it an explicit goal. Some researchers of top-performing athletes call this feature 'inner arrogance', and we believe the term applies to athletic leaders as well.

Ambition (some scholars use the more politically correct term, 'belief in ability to win') makes athletic leaders consider difficult tasks as challenges to be mastered rather than threats to be avoided. They set challenging goals and maintain a strong commitment to them; they sustain effort in the face of failure; and they quickly restore a sense of efficacy after setbacks. It is interesting that all four of the leaders we studied (with some caveats in the case of Kaspersky) were industry outsiders, yet each of them demonstrated a high level of confidence from his earliest days in the job onwards. Saveliev, Aeroflot's CEO, spoke to his team about turning the company into the airline of choice for European travellers only a few weeks after taking the job.

Passion

Fetisov, the many-time Olympic and world champion and captain of the famous 'Red Machine' USSR ice hockey team in the 1980s told us that 'you cannot keep winning, playing or training beyond the pain barrier for money – you have to love it!'[9]

Sergey Galitsky, the founder and CEO of the largest retail chain in Russia, Magnit, said in one of his rare interviews, 'Energy a person spend on something always results in quality. If you are a businessman, you should think about business all the time – that is how you will win.'[10]

---

[9] In interview with authors.
[10] V. Kozlov, 'Galitsky', *Expert-Yug* 220 (2012): 28–31.

The leaders we studied are passionate about their business, the organizations they head and people they lead. They speak about them with enthusiasm, devote most of their time to them, and willingly accept minor and major suffering for them. Passion gives them motivation, energy and focus.

Focus

A focus on performance and total concentration are the cornerstones of daily life, training and competition for top athletes. A number of recent studies show that they have powerful strategies for getting back on track fast when their level of performance drops or external distractions get in the way. Athletic leaders demonstrate the same exceptional level of concentration and focus. Bombarded with myriad ideas, requests and demands on their time, they stay centred on a limited number of priorities, which they pursue with unparalleled passion.

Oleg Bagrin, the CEO of NLMK, an international steelmaker with assets in Russia, the United States, the European Union (EU) and India, explained to us that for the last four years his focus had been on improving the group's profitability through operational effectiveness – and he did just that, in spite of multiple alternatives that came his way. As a result of his concentration and organizational focus the company's profitability (ratio of EBITDA to revenue) grew from 11 per cent to 25 per cent.

A focused mindset allows leaders to work with issues they cannot control, block out distractions, minimize stress when things are not perfect and, most importantly, keep their organizations concentrated on a few key issues. One Gazprom Neft executive describes CEO Dyukov as a man who 'when he decides on something will make sure you do that, no matter what'.[11]

Cool-headedness

Passion fires up athletic leaders, but just like athletic champions, they master their emotions when the time comes to make important decisions or negotiate significant deals. Keeping a 'cool head'

---

[11] In interview with authors.

means that a leader has a strong ability to stay calm and think clearly under very stressful conditions. A leader with a cool head applies logic to the situation, analyses available data, seeks expert advice, considers different options and synthesizes a solution.

In 2009, just a few months after becoming Aeroflot's CEO, Saveliev made the controversial decision to take 26 TU-154 airplanes out of service. The company was in very bad shape and every rouble of revenue counted. Many company veterans asked him to reconsider, but the new CEO stayed firm. Mathematical analysis subsequently proved that, because of very low fuel efficiency, every TU-154 flight added US$10,000 to US$20,000 to the company's losses. Similarly, when Alexander decided not only to move Gazprom Neft's headquarters to St Petersburg from Moscow but also to relocate all key people there, most Gazprom Neft executives were sceptical and some tried to persuade the CEO to lower his ambitions, but the move took place as planned. Most key people were still working in St Petersburg four years later.

Mercilessness

High-achievement sport requires athletes to go beyond what is considered possible for human beings. It involves enormous mental and physical pressure – even at times pain and physical injury. Studies show that top athletes are ready to subject their bodies and brains to strenuous exercise, despite knowing that this may result in injuries, illnesses and loss of some important functions. Rasmus Ankersen, a bestselling author and expert in high performance in sport, gives many examples of athletes working beyond what is considered possible for a human being. He quotes one European long-distance runner: 'Here (in Kenya) I see runners suffer to a degree that I cannot in my wildest dreams imagine anybody in the West subjecting themselves to. This is a fast moving journey which wrenches the body beyond its moral limitations: it starts with the recognition that pain is the validation of accomplishment.'[12] As well as being merciless to themselves, champions do not spare their support teams – not to mention their competitors.

[12] R. Ankersen, *The Golden Mine Effect: Crack the Secrets of High Performance* (London: Icon Publishing, 2011).

Athletic Leaders are similar. Herman Gref of Sberbank sleeps five hours a day, runs 10 miles in the morning and works until very late at night. He expects other Sberbank executives to work just as hard. But a leader's mercilessness is not only about the number and intensity of their working hours; it also translates into demanding standards of behaviour, extremely challenging goals and zero tolerance towards low performance and mediocrity. In the nine years that Gref has been working for Sberbank, half of his management board members have left the company. One of them explained, 'It was great to work with him, but after five years I felt completely exhausted. I just could not carry on.'[13] Galitsky, whose purchasing managers are known as the toughest negotiators in the industry, likes to repeat, 'In business the same as in sport, a very important skill is the ability to finish off [your competitors].'[14]

To assess your mental toughness, please refer to the Table 1.1.

Mental Adaptability

We would particularly like to emphasize three elements of adaptability which have a strong impact on athletic leaders' agendas and actual behaviour: proactive curiosity, rapid knowledge reinvigoration and flexible mental models.

Proactive Curiosity

Academics disagree about curiosity. Is it a motive or driver, the explanation of a specific behaviour, or a behaviour itself? For the purposes of our leadership model and the following discussion we treat 'proactive curiosity' as a personality trait of athletic leaders, which results in specific repetitive behaviours. Our protagonists demonstrate what Cicero called a 'passion for learning' in relation to their businesses and leadership projects, and many other subjects besides. Almost every meeting we had in carrying out our research for this book started with a question from our interviewees: 'What's new in your part of the world?' Saveliev always asked about our last experience of flying Aeroflot,

---

[13] In interview with authors.
[14] Sergey Galitsky, Official Twitter account, @sergeygalitskiy.

Table 1.1   Reflection: How Tough Is Your Mind?

Rate yourself

Ambition

A. Goals that I set for myself look unrealistic and unachievable to other people

Very much like me	5
Like me	4
Neutral	3
Unlike me	2
Very much unlike me	1

B. I believe that there is no need to set a bar which is too high for myself and others

Very much like me	1
Like me	2
Neutral	3
Unlike me	4
Very much unlike me	5

Composite score A and B: _____

Passion

A. My business is the main thing that drives me

Very much like me	5
Like me	4
Neutral	3
Unlike me	2
Very much unlike me	1

B. I am not ready to dedicate most of my time to my job

Very much like me	1
Like me	2
Neutral	3
Unlike me	4
Very much unlike me	5

Composite score A and B: _____

Focus

A. I can easily describe my two to three main priorities at this moment

Very much like me	5
Like me	4
Neutral	3
Unlike me	2
Very much unlike me	1

B. I prefer not to have firm plans and usually base my activity on the current situation

Very much like me	1
Like me	2

Table 1.1   (*Continued*)

Rate yourself

Neutral	3
Unlike me	4
Very much unlike me	5

Composite score A and B: _____

Cool-headedness

A. *In difficult or stressful situations people often look at me as a person who can resolve them*

Very much like me	5
Like me	4
Neutral	3
Unlike me	2
Very much unlike me	1

B. *Usually I need time to make a correct decision under pressure*

Very much like me	1
Like me	2
Neutral	3
Unlike me	4
Very much unlike me	5

Composite score A and B: _____

Mercilessness

A. *I believe that achievement involves sweat and tears*

Very much like me	5
Like me	4
Neutral	3
Unlike me	2
Very much unlike me	1

B. *I think tension and stress are signs that you are doing something wrong at work*

Very much like me	1
Like me	2
Neutral	3
Unlike me	4
Very much unlike me	5

Composite score A and B: _____

What have you learned about yourself while completing this exercise?

_____

_____

_____

_____

and Dyukov enquired about the situation in France and Western Europe.

This interest in discovery leads to questions, meetings with people from different areas of expertise, study trips, and reading books and articles. Athletic leaders are willing to take the risk of appearing incompetent or ignorant in order to make a discovery. They are proactive in their search for knowledge and never take a break from this journey. Gref, who is reputed to be Russia's number one business leader for learning, reads about 300 books a year, regularly goes to Silicon Valley to explore business and technology innovation, attends conferences, asks questions and listens, listens and listens to people from all over the world. Proactive curiosity makes investigation an integral part of an athletic leader's life both at work and off work. It creates a continuous inflow of new information, which in turn leads to a continuous development of their knowledge base. All people learn as they go through their careers and lives, but athletic leaders learn and unlearn exceptionally fast.

Rapid Knowledge Reinvigoration

In the twenty-first century, CEOs are first and foremost knowledge workers. We know from research that knowledge obsolescence is one of the major challenges for contemporary professionals, and CEOs are no exception. Athletic leaders deal with this challenge by constantly and rapidly acquiring new knowledge and disposing of outdated information. Their knowledge base is continuously evolving – and fast. This happens because their proactive curiosity is complemented by a conscious process of updating their knowledge, which takes multiple forms.

Saveliev entered civil aviation – an industry known for its technical sophistication – at the age of 56 without any insider knowledge. He immediately set up a 'Saturday school' – a weekly workshop with consultants to learn about aviation. In just six months, he reached the same standard as veteran Aeroflot executives. And within two years he knew enough to develop Aeroflot's new strategy. Today, other airline CEOs seek his advice on industry matters. Gref, who had never been a banker before joining Sberbank, became an industry authority in three years, a black belt in lean production in a year and an authority on the digital economy less than two years after first encountering the topic.

Rapid learning has enabled our athletic leaders to accomplish what most CEOs fail to do: achieve sustainable superior performance in an industry that is completely new to them. Tinkov did so no less than three times – in food production, brewing and banking.

Flexible Mental Models

Athletic leaders not only constantly update their knowledge base and adopt new skills and techniques but also their adaptability also allows them to adjust their mental models – their internal explanations of how the world and its component parts function. Their mental representations of their businesses, industries and countries – and the global environments in which all of these operate – evolve all the time, allowing new strategic approaches to emerge. Research shows that most CEOs remain 'one trick ponies' for the duration of their tenure and that inflexible mental models become their major handicap when the world moves ahead. Athletic leaders do not suffer from this disease.

According to Saveliev, when he entered Aeroflot his view of civil aviation was crystal clear – 'it's a service business'. The customer was king, and the airline had to focus on the customer. His 'Saturday school' lessons soon made him adjust that mental model – civil aviation is also about capacity utilization and operational effectiveness. His next big move was to view the industry as a playing field for two competing business models: 'low-cost airline' and 'premium carrier'. Then he adjusted his mindset to see it as a battleground for airline groups catering to the whole market rather than to certain segments. Adapting mental models in this way had a direct impact on Saveliev's actions and Aeroflot's strategy. Initially the airline invested in customer care, then became a premium service provider and later built a portfolio of carriers including the most dynamic low-cost airline in Europe, Pobeda.

Gref's mental evolution was even more spectacular. In less than a decade his world view changed from that of an increasingly interconnected global system to an ecosystem of country organisms competing and collaborating at the same time. Gref's mental representation of banks evolved from 'institutions forming the cornerstone of the global and national economies' to 'organizations of the past, which will be wiped out by the digital economy'. The initial strategy of 'building a world-class financial institution' through superb customer care, investment in human capital and high operational efficiency gave way to 'building a digital company.'

To assess your mental adaptability, please refer to the Table 1.2.

Context and Leadership Challenges

Since the work of Paul Hersey and Ken Blanchard,[15] the context in which leaders operate has become an important element of every leadership model. The case of athletic leaders is no different. They operate in a specific context, which modifies the traditional leadership functions defined by Max Weber: setting direction; developing action plans; instituting norms; creating mechanisms of coordination and control; and mobilizing resources.[16] Instead, their role is to rise to distinctive challenges that may be non-existent or insignificant in the better-researched contexts of developed market economies. Saveliev of Aeroflot has to ensure that citizens of Russia's Far East have access to air transportation (the only way of travelling for the major part of the region), although this service makes no economic sense for his publicly traded company. Kaspersky deals with an intellectual property protection mechanism that is virtually non-existent in Russia on a daily basis. Gref of Sberbank could not send his key managers to attend courses at top business schools because most of them did not speak English. And Dyukov of Gazprom Neft expects government regulations to change any time.

In our model we make a distinction between the macrocontext – global, country and industry – and the microcontext of the company. Both create constraints and opportunities for leaders

---

[15] P. Hersey and K. H. Blanchard, *Management of Organizational Behavior: Utilizing Human Resources* (Englewood Cliffs, NJ: Prentice Hall, 1969).

[16] M. Weber, *The Theory of Social and Economic Organization* (New York: Free Press, 1964).

Table 1.2 How Adaptable Is Your Mind?

Rate yourself

Proactive curiosity

A. *People around me consider me insatiable for new knowledge*
Very much like me	5
Like me	4
Neutral	3
Unlike me	2
Very much unlike me	1

B. *Sometimes I can't decide what to read or explore*
Very much like me	1
Like me	2
Neutral	3
Unlike me	4
Very much unlike me	5

Composite score A and B: _____

Rapid knowledge reinvigoration

A. *I never get tired of improving my skills and becoming familiar with new technologies*
Very much like me	5
Like me	4
Neutral	3
Unlike me	2
Very much unlike me	1

B. *I miss the times when a basic qualification was enough for professional success*
Very much like me	1
Like me	2
Neutral	3
Unlike me	4
Very much unlike me	5

Composite score A and B: _____

Flexible mental models

A. *I consider myself flexible in my opinions and beliefs*
Very much like me	5
Like me	4
Neutral	3
Unlike me	2
Very much unlike me	1

B. *It is difficult for me to change my mind*
Very much like me	1

(continued)

Table 1.2   (*Continued*)

Rate yourself	
Like me	2
Neutral	3
Unlike me	4
Very much unlike me	5

Composite score A and B: _____

What have you learned about yourself while completing this exercise?

_____

_____

_____

_____

and influence their agendas and practices. Synthesizing our conversations with the protagonists of the book (and hundreds of other leaders) and building on limited research into the contemporary Russian business context, we have identified a number of key characteristics of each of them.

It is very hard to describe the complexity of the macro-environment of athletic leaders in a sentence or two. Multiple factors have a direct and indirect impact on their agendas, actions and results. Fully aware of the risk of oversimplification, we would like to emphasize four salient characteristics of their wider environment: *rapid change and knowledge obsolescence; turbulence; heavy government interference;* and *the high-power distance cultural leadership tradition.*

The first of these trends is global and, to varying degrees, affects all businesses in the world. Because of the large size of the companies the athletic leaders manage and the global nature of their industries, it has a strong and ever-increasing impact, creating a *challenge of staying current and competitive* with respect to products, technologies, processes and business models. This trend is well documented and researched, so we devote our limited pages to describing other – more subtle – characteristics of the context for athletic leadership. Readers who would like to learn more about knowledge obsolescence can look at 'Adaptability: The New Competitive Advantage', by M. Reeves and M. Deimler; 'Be

Figure 1.3 Russia's Year-to-Year GDP Dynamics (2004–16).

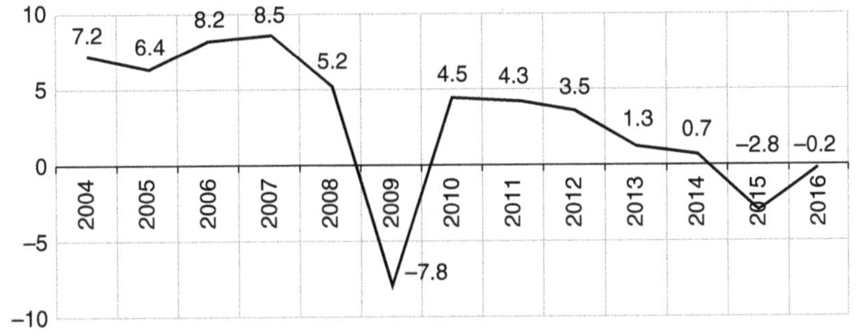

Source: World Bank.

Forewarned: Your Knowledge Is Decaying', by S. Arbesman; and 'Why Good Companies Go Bad', by D. Sull.

The word 'turbulent' comes from the Latin *turba*, which means confusion. Modern dictionaries define turbulent as 'not stable or calm', 'characterized by disorder', 'full of upheavals' and 'involving a lot of sudden changes'. Even a cursory look at Russia's economy and its relationships with the rest of the world over the last decade reveals all of these characteristics (see Figures 1.3–1.4 and Insert, 'The Russian Roller Coaster'.)

Turbulence creates a lot of challenges for business leaders. It makes it difficult to execute such important leadership roles as planning, evaluating and rewarding, and undermines traditional business tools like annual plans, budgets and performance reviews. A CEO of a Russian company explained to us, 'My board is very unhappy that for the last four years our actual results are far off our business plans. They criticize management for poor planning and a lack of forecasting skills. But how could I forecast accurately when every year I have a few black swans landing in my pond?'[17] In fact turbulence challenges the ability of managers to perform their core leadership function, which is to reduce uncertainty for their followers by painting an attractive and convincing picture of the future.

[17] In interview with authors.

Figure 1.4 Bank of Russia Key Rate (2003–17).
The Bank of Russia key rate was introduced on 3 March 2014. We use the weekly rate of repo auctions as the closest analogue for the period before 2014.

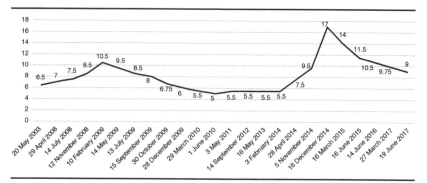

Source: The Central Bank of the Russian Federation (Bank of Russia).

The Russian Roller Coaster

In 2001, in the aftermath of 9/11, Russian president Vladimir Putin offered his US counterpart, George W. Bush, full support and assistance in combating terrorism. Russia's relationships with the West reached an all-time high; economic, cultural, technological, political and military cooperation flourished. Western banks became major lenders to Russian private companies, BP formed a US$30 billion joint venture with Russian entrepreneurs, and Russia turned into the second-largest market for global oilfield services provider Schlumberger. Latvia, Estonia and Lithuania's accession to NATO in 2004 irritated Putin but did not lead to any retaliation. When, in a 2007 speech in Munich, he warned NATO against inviting Georgia and Ukraine to join, Western leaders noticed the change in tone. In 2008, the short war with Georgia dealt another blow to Russia's relationships with the West. Re-elected to his third term in 2012, President Putin began to talk about a multipolar world and turned his attention towards Asia. The Russian annexation of Crimea in 2014 led to economic sanctions from the United States, the EU and other developed economies as well as Russia's ejection from the Group of 8 (G8). Events in Eastern Ukraine triggered new sanctions and took relationships between Russia and the West to an all-time post-USSR low. In addition, Russia's support for President Bashar al-Assad and military intervention in Syria strained its relationship with Turkey. The downing of a

Russian military plane by a Turkish missile provoked a war of words between the Turkish and Russian presidents and caused Russian economic sanctions to be swiftly revoked after the former apologized to the latter. Russia and Turkey finally saw eye to eye again. After years of passive Asian policy, Russia in 2013 signed a multi-billion-dollar contract to supply China with natural gas. President Putin called the country its 'new strategic partner'.

Turbulence is not a uniquely Russian characteristic. Many industries and countries experience instability and unpredictable change. In Russia's case, its impact on business leaders is amplified by another salient characteristic of the environment: *heavy government intervention.*

Government plays an important role in shaping the business environment by adopting laws, imposing taxes and providing services such as infrastructure, education, health care and security in every country. In contemporary Russia's case, its influence goes beyond these traditional roles. Its presence is heavy both in terms of the scale of the intervention and often the style: arbitrary and brutal. The Russian government controls a large share of the national economy – more than 60 per cent of gross domestic product (GDP). It also has an active corporate presence. The combined revenue of the largest 28 state-owned Russian companies represents more than half of the combined revenue of the top 100 Russian companies and has kept growing steadily since 2008. State-owned enterprises dominate such important sectors as transport, banking, shipbuilding and aerospace. On top of taxes and direct business activities the Russian government actively interferes in business through economic and criminal investigations. In the last five years such government bodies as the General Prosecutors' Office and the Investigative Committee have significantly increased their level of activity. As a result the number of bankruptcies in Russia more than doubled between 2007 and 2015. More and more business people are receiving prison terms for 'economic crimes'.

In addition to traditional forms of government intervention in the economy, Russian business leaders have to deal with subtler informal methods. It is not uncommon for a CEO of a Russian company to receive a request from a governor to build a swimming pool or to pave a local road. He may be encouraged or advised not to take part in a bidding for a specific government contract or asked to make sure that all his employees vote in the next election. Some government officials are directly involved in business through companies owned by their family members or frontmen, and use their influence to facilitate their businesses' work. Cases of corporate raiding orchestrated by businessmen with the help of government officials are quite common in Russia. In spite of government anti-corruption efforts, bribery by government officials remains widespread and is taking on more sophisticated forms.

Business leaders in Russia have to face omnipresent and multifaceted government and government officials who often combine their day jobs with shadow entrepreneurship. According to a CEO of an energy company, 'You don't know when or how the government will hit you, but you know it will.' 'I spend at least 30 per cent of my time working on government-related or, more accurately, government-provoked issues,'[18] he continued. Specifically government-related leadership challenges in Russia include navigating a complex and often contradictory maze of Russian legislation; protecting business from hostile takeovers; defending business from special taxes, levies or fines imposed by the government; and maintaining productive relationships with government officials at different levels and with different government bodies that are often competing for influence and other resources.

Russia is not the only country where the government is heavily involved in business in multiple roles and forms. Many emerging economies like China, Brazil and Turkey have recently experienced a surge in government intervention. Globally, industries such as aviation, banking, mining, oil and gas, and, more recently, the Internet experience high levels of regulation and direct government involvement. The challenges we mention here are not unique to Russia.

Leadership is a relationship that exists in a specific social and cultural context. Athletic leaders are operating at the beginning of the twenty-first century, and global trends such as digitalization,

---

[18] In interview with authors.

the rise of social media, concerns for sustainability and the environment, and the humanization of professional relationships are having a noticeable impact on them and their leadership. At the same time, they are working in Russia, a country with its own deep leadership tradition, which also creates constraints and opportunities for them.

We often conduct the following exercise with the participants of executive development workshops. First, we ask them to close their eyes and to share with the group what they perceive when the instructor says the word 'leadership'. With minor exceptions, the resulting free associations are similar among Russian participants from different industries, types of companies and age groups – and have remained consistent during the 20 years in which we have been doing this exercise. The most common images are of 'a strong tall man', 'Stalin, Lenin, Putin', 'a general', 'the leader of a pack of wolves', 'an ocean liner', 'a racing car', 'Everest' and so on. In essence, there is a picture of a man (almost all associations are of masculine gender in the Russian language) who stands high and alone, sees far and exhibits confidence. We described the Russian leadership tradition in detail in our book *The New Russian Business Leaders*,[19] but we would like to repeat some of its key features here. Traditional Russian leadership is the following:

Vertical
> The hierarchy is strict, obedience to superiors is expected and reinforced, and subordinates have inferior status and accept it. The short formula 'sucking up, bullying down' captures the essence of this aspect.

Relationships Based Rather Than Rules Based
> Leaders have their own rules, and the rules for subordinates may change with no notice. Different rules apply to different people, depending on how close they are to the leader. Different contexts call for different rules and norms.

---

[19] M. F. E. Kets de Vries, S. Shekshnia, K. Korotov and E. Florent-Treacy, *The New Russian Business Leaders: New Horizons in Leadership Studies* (Cheltenham, UK: Edward Elgar Publishing, 2004).

Short Term and Problem Focused Rather Than Long Term and Opportunities Driven

The Russian nation emerged under very harsh conditions of severe climate, infertile land and low natural protection from multiple external enemies, so daily survival became a major preoccupation for the whole population, including its leaders. The latter still think about immediate results, are uncomfortable with long-term projects and prefer to avoid mistakes rather than bet on big wins.

Emotional

Although to some foreigners Russians seem to be cold and even poker-faced, leadership is an emotional business for latter. Russian leaders are expected to care about their business and their followers – and to demonstrate passion. Raising voices, slamming fists on the table and intimidating others with jokes and criticisms are all elements of a leader's routine.

Magic

In the Russian leadership tradition, people are ready to accept their leaders' domination and follow them without question, because they attribute almost superhuman qualities to their bosses and expect them to deliver miracles from time to time. Miracles can take the shape of winning a very lucrative contract, receiving a medal from the president or simply scoring five times during the company team's ice hockey game.

As our little experiments and more structured research show, the traditional Russian leadership model has a strong impact on how contemporary Russians perceive leader–follower dynamics and behave. This creates specific challenges such as engaging followers who are used to executing orders in autonomous, meaningful and innovative work; motivating them to dream beyond pure survival; delegating authority and resources; getting subordinates to accept responsibility for their performance, development and advancement; and introducing effective company-wide policies and procedures. The CEO of a telecom company put it this way: 'My employees often remind me of my children. They want you to decide where to go, to take them there, to entertain them on the way – and they will blame you (behind your back) if they did not like the place.'[20]

Although the traditional Russian leadership model is probably the most specific element of the macroenvironment of athletic leaders, many emerging countries, for example, Turkey, Nigeria, China and Vietnam, have somewhat similar hierarchical, relationships-based models of leader–follower interaction embedded in their collective subconscious. Business leaders there face similar challenges and may apply similar solutions.

The three characteristics of turbulence, heavy government involvement and the vertical leadership tradition make the macrocontext in which athletic leaders operate distinct and specific, and have a direct influence on their agendas and practices. Some elements of the microcontext are also similar for all of them and have an impact on their leadership.

All of the four men we studied began their leadership journeys from *a relatively low base*. Although Sberbank was the largest bank in Russia in 2008, both in terms of number of customers and size of assets, it was inefficient, notorious for poor service and technologically obsolete. When Saveliev joined Aeroflot, the company was bleeding cash, losing market share and stuck with gas-guzzling planes. Kaspersky started with a three-man cooperative. In each of our protagonists' industries, there were companies more advanced and successful than theirs. This allowed for fast, intensive learning and the borrowing of ideas and practices.

At the same time, each of them had *a full mandate* for action from a key stakeholder: Gref and Saveliev from the Russian president; Dyukov from Gazprom's CEO, Alexey Miller; and Kaspersky from himself. The leaders did not have to worry (at least initially) about multiple stakeholders and their expectations, and could press ahead with ambitious programmes.

Last but not least, our athletic leaders headed organizations whose employees, on average, lacked modern-day skills, especially *management competency and a strong work ethic*. In the words of Gref, 'Most of Sberbank's middle managers went to college during the 1990s – the lowest point in the history of Russian education. They

---

[20] In interview with authors.

did not receive proper education, and the bank has to compensate for it.'[21] The relatively low quality of human capital became a serious constraint for the athletic leaders but also allowed them to shape their employees' skills and attitudes to their own tastes.

In summary, we have synthesized five metachallenges that athletic leaders have to deal with – and that strongly influence what they do and how they do it:

- staying ahead of the game in a world where products, technologies and business models are becoming obsolete with ever-increasing speed
- navigating the maze of an extremely turbulent environment
- building world-class companies with second-rate human capital
- maintaining leadership legitimacy in the eyes of diverse stake-holders with high expectations
- effectively dealing with an omnipresent government.

What Athletic Leaders Are Not

We felt that another way to describe athletic leadership to the reader would be to write about what athletic CEOs *are not*. During the last two decades we saw a strong trend in the leadership literature to construct an effective leader as a positive, emotionally intelligent, servant, coaching executive. Some scholars propose a model of *positive*, or positively deviant leadership, when leaders promote interpersonal flourishing, well-being at work, positive emotions and flow in organizations they lead.[22] *Strength-based leadership* constructs the image of leaders, who discover and develop strengths and abilities of their employees.[23] The image

---

[21] In interview with authors.

[22] K. Cameron, *Positive Leadership. Strategies for Extraordinary Performance* (San Francisco: Barrett-Koehler Publishers, 2008); B. Fredrickson, *Positivity* (Brunswick, OH: Crown Custom Publishing, 2009), L. P. Wooten and K. Cameron, 'Enablers of a Positive Strategy: Positively Deviant Leadership', in *The Oxford Handbook of Positive Psychology and Work*, ed. P. A. Linley, S. Harrington and N. Garcea (Oxford: Oxford University Press, 2013), 53–67.

[23] M. Buckingham and D. O. Clifton, *Now, Discover Your Strengths* (New York: Free Press, 2002); D. Cooperrider, D. Whitney, J. M. Stavros and R. Fry, *The*

of a *leader as coach*, who helps followers discover and develop their potential, has become very popular both in academic and practitioner-oriented literature.[24] The *servant leadership* model describes a leader who cares about followers, turns the power pyramid upside down, listens to employees, and builds trust and foresight.[25] Models of *emotional leadership* emphasize leaders' competency to recognize, understand and manage personal and other people's emotions as the core of effective leadership.[26] Most of them are rather idealistic and normative, and describe what effectiveleadershipshouldlooklikeratherwhatitlookslikeinreality. They make an important contribution to the development of new discourses in leadership science and to constructing new forms of leadership personality and behaviour. The model of athletic leadership allows to capture the practice of leadership. It describes what effective leadership actually looks like in the specific context, defined by rapid obsolescence, high turbulence, heavy government involvement, high-power distance leadership tradition and a relatively low starting base. This model is ambivalent because it reflects both 'good' and 'bad' sides of leadership. Some specific elements of athletic leadership go against well-established and widely accepted leadership models. We would like to give two examples of such incongruence to shed extra light on what athletic CEOs are not.

Athletic leaders are not 'Level Five' leaders as depicted in Jim Collins's bestselling book *From Good to Great*.[27] They are

Appreciative Inquiry Handbook: For Leaders of Change (Brunswick, OH: Crown Custom Publishing, 2008); P. H. Brun, D. Cooperrider and M. Ejsing, *Strengths-Based Leadership Handbook* (Brunswick, OH: Crown Custom Publishing, 2016).

[24] J. Whitmore, *Coaching for Performance: GROWing Human Potential and Purpose – The Principles and Practice of Coaching and Leadership* (London: Nicholas Brealey Publishing, 2009); J. M. Kouzes and B. Z. Posner, 'When Leaders Are Coaches', in *Coaching for Leadership: The Practice of Leadership Coaching from the World's Greatest Coaches*, ed. M. Goldsmith and L. Lyons (San Francisco: Pfeiffer, 2006), 136–45.

[25] L. C. Spears and M. Lawrence (eds), Practicing Servant-Leadership: Succeeding Through Trust, Bravery, and Forgiveness (San Francisco: Jossey-Bass, 2004).

[26] D. Goleman, R. Boyatzis and A. McKee, *Primal Leadership: Realizing the Power of Emotional Intelligence* (Boston: Harvard Business School, 2002).

[27] J. C. Collins, *Good to Great: Why Some Companies Make the Leap ... and Others Don't* (New York: HarperBusiness, 2001).

not humble but openly ambitious. Often they do not separate organizational and personal ambition, but it does not follow that the latter is lacking. They say 'I' much more often than 'we'. They do not follow 'the Window and the Mirror' pattern that Collins describes; rather, they habitually take the credit for success and may blame subordinates for underperformance. They set themselves very high standards, which they also apply to their followers. They usually decide on a course of action and only then think about the people who will carry it out (contravening the 'First Who ... Then What' principle of 'Level Five' leaders). They do not shy away from the limelight but constantly seek it. Saveliev appears in every issue of the Aeroflot inflight magazine, and Gref has given more than a hundred press interviews since becoming Sberbank CEO.

Athletic leaders do not demonstrate another recognized attribute of effective leadership: *emotional intelligence* – at least not in the way described by Peter Salovey, John Mayer, David Caruso or Daniel Goleman, who write about understanding and regulating personal emotions, understanding the emotions of other people and interacting with them on the basis of that awareness.[28] Athletic leaders are relaxed about managing their own emotions and give themselves the freedom to raise their voices, humiliate or threaten followers. They criticize more often than they praise. Providing positive, constructive feedback is not their strongest competency. One of them said to us, 'My deputies are mature, well-paid professionals – if they don't understand what they do well, they should not be where they are. They don't need feedback.'[29] Athletic leaders do not often reflect on what effect their actions and words have on other people and rarely take any steps to correct negative outcomes. They are so passionate about what they do that they assume others share the same passion, demonstrate the same level of commitment and therefore do not require any kid-glove treatment. Like top athletes, athletic

---

[28] D. R. Caruso and P. Salovey, *The Emotionally Intelligent Manager* (San Francisco: Jossey-Bass, 2004); D. Goleman, *Emotional Intelligence: Why It Can Matter More Than IQ* (New York: Bantam Books, 1995).

[29] In interview with authors.

leaders are so concentrated on winning that they tend to forget about the people who help them win. In a characteristic episode, Kaspersky, dressed in a Hawaiian shirt, jeans and sneakers, greeted a delegation of INSEAD MBA candidates at his office with 'I have only 20 minutes for you and I don't give a damn about how I am dressed.' Then he spent an hour and a half talking about his company and global Internet security, before giving them a tour of the company's museum.

It is important to add that passionate and dynamic athletic leaders find calm, patience, flexibility and self-restraint when dealing with superiors. They can wait for hours to meet with the Russian president, quietly listen to monologues from top government officials and smile at the bad jokes of VIPs. As we will see, this quality translates into very tangible business results.

Further Reading

Arbesman, A. 'Be Forewarned: Your Knowledge is Decaying', *Harvard Business Review*, 5 November 2012.

Beer, M., Eisenstat, R. A., Foote, N., Fredberg, T. and Norrgren, F. *Higher Ambition: How Great Leaders Create Economic and Social Value*. Boston: Harvard Business School Press, 2011.

Brooks, D. *The Road to Character*. New York: Random House, 2015.

Duckworth, A. *Grit: Why Passion and Resilience Are the Secrets to Success*. London: Vermilion, 2016.

Dweck, C. *Mindset: The New Psychology of Success*. New York: Random House, 2006.

Ericsson, K. A. (ed.). *The Road to Excellence: The Acquisition of Expert Performance in the Arts and Sciences, Sports, and Games*. Mahweh, NJ: Erlbaum, 1996.

Grant, A. Originals: How Non-Conformists Move the World. New York: Viking, 2016.

Gucciardi, D. F., and Gordon, S. (eds). *Mental Toughness in Sport: Developments in Theory and Research*. Abingdon, Oxon: Routledge, 2011.

Harrell, E. 'How 1% Performance Improvements Led to Olympic Gold', *Harvard Business Review*, 30 October 2015.

Haslam, S. A., Reicher, S. D. and Platow, M. J. *The New Psychology of Leadership: Identity, Influence and Power*. New York: Psychology Press, 2011.

Nye, J. S. Jr. *The Powers to Lead*. New York: Oxford University Press, 2008.

Reeves, M., and Deimler, M. 'Adaptability: The New Competitive Advantage', *Harvard Business Review*, July–August 2011.

Taylor, B. 'Why Sports Are a Terrible Metaphor for Business', *Harvard Business Review*, 3 February 2017.

Westerbeek, H., and Smith, A. *Business Leadership and the Lessons from Sport*. New York: Palgrave Macmillan, 2005.

Films and Television Series

I Am Bolt. Documentary film directed by Benjamin Turner and Gabe Turner. London: Fullwell 73, Doyen Global, 2016.

Pelé: Birth of a Legend. Film directed by Jeff Zimbalist and Michael Zimbalist. Beverly Hills: Imagine Entertainment, 2016.

Red Army. Documentary film directed by Gabe Polsky. Los Angeles: Gabriel Polsky Productions; Los Angeles: Imagine Entertainment, 2014.

When We Were Kings. Documentary film directed by Leon Gast. Santa Monica, CA: PolyGram Filmed Entertainment, 1996.

2

The Agenda and Practices of Athletic Leaders

The purpose of training is to tighten up the slack, toughen the body, and polish the spirit.

— *Morihei Ueshiba, Aikido founder*

You miss 100% of the shots you never take.

— *Wayne Gretzky*

Leadership Agenda

The goals and objectives of each athletic leader are highly specific – and to a large degree determined by the company they lead and the industry it operates in. Alexander Dyukov wants Gazprom Neft to be the best in class in terms of operational efficiency and health, safety and environmental (HSE) protection. Vitaly Saveliev strives to make Aeroflot one of the top 20 airlines by number of passengers and the most profitable in terms of return on equity. Herman Gref is building a digital organization that will provide a whole range of services to hundreds of millions of private and corporate customers, including banking. Yet there are some striking commonalities in their *leadership agendas*: the ambitions and major themes that guide their leadership action.

The agendas of athletic leaders are complex and multidimensional, with many different overarching themes, time horizons and specific projects. However, there are two central leitmotifs in all this diversity: *winning and transforming* (see Table 2.1).

Table 2.1   Sample Athletic Leader's Agenda for 2017 and Beyond

Priority	Timescale	Metrics	Projects
Dealing another blow to competitor A	First quarter	Market share – 5 per cent gain from them	Product Z New sales incentive policy Sales improvement programme
Improving operational efficiency of back office	Next 12 months	Back office cost as a percentage of revenue down 15 per cent	New operating system IT investment Employee assessment Benchmarking trips to global leaders
Bringing capacity utilization to the level of best in class	Next 18 months	Reaching 85 per cent capacity utilization on a year-round basis	Appointing director for capacity management Applying big data techniques to capacity management KPIs for all business unit heads
Creating an agile organization	Next 24 months	Time to market for new products increased by 2,000 per cent	IT platform Agile manual for the company Agile incubator
Joining top-five global league	Next 48 months	Among five largest companies in the world in the industry in terms of revenue Global presence Highest return on assets in the industry (among large players)	International M&A programme Asset replacement investment programme 'Leader 2020' management development programme 'Innovation 2020' performance enhancement programme
Improving quality of governance in the regions where we operate	Next 36 months	Our regions to be in the top 20 according to annual government ranking Reduction in 'invited' company charitable contributions by 50 per cent	'Effective Regional Manager' executive development programme for vice governors and regional ministers in cooperation with State Academy of National Economy and Government Service Seconding company managers to regional administrations 'Effective regional governance' fund
Mastering 'scrum' project management	First quarter	I can do it myself	Attend a workshop Read a book

Like top-performing athletes, athletic leaders are determined to win. We will see later how this goal (or, rather, attitude) translates into specific leadership practices. For now, it is enough to note that these leaders are very competitive and want to win on multiple fronts. First, they want to beat specific competitors – companies and leaders that they recognize as such. Some are open about this, while others keep the names and criteria to themselves, but they all have such rivals – which may not necessarily come from the same industry. In fact, some of our protagonists compete with each other. One of their deputies told us, 'Sberbank is both a benchmark and a rival for us. Our boss constantly follows up on what's going on there and feels good when we do something better.'[1]

Second, athletic leaders work hard to beat their own records. They want their companies to constantly outperform themselves. Vadim Yakovlev, vice president at Gazprom Neft, says, 'Dyukov sets the bar higher and higher for himself and the organization, even if market conditions or the board of directors do not require that to happen.'[2] He adds that this goal-setting approach 'makes every manager in the company constantly think about becoming better and look for ways to improve or to do things completely differently. It sets into motion the whole culture of superior performance.'[3] All of our athletic leaders are fanatics of performance monitoring and make their followers also be fanatical about this. For example, Saveliev equipped 90 Aeroflot executives with so-called management monitors – iPads providing access to 427 operational and financial indicators in real time. The CEO himself never parts with his device, as if it were his 'nuclear key', and starts his day by opening it while still in bed.

Third, athletic leaders do not rest on their domestic laurels. They are determined to play and win in the top league, so their benchmarks are global and they go after the best in their industries. Back in 1997, young Kaspersky, who had no money, organization or sales channels, set himself and his small team a clear goal: to be the best in the world in antivirus protection software.

---

[1] In interview with authors.
[2] In interview with authors.
[3] In interview with authors.

Since then he has not lowered the bar. Similarly, Dyukov set Gazprom Neft the target of catching up with Shell and BP's HSE performance and operational efficiency within five years, even though his company is already a leader in the Russian market. This attitude adds such important projects as global market and competitor intelligence and continuous benchmarking to athletic leaders' agendas. For example, Aeroflot employees regularly fly with competitor airlines and submit detailed reports to management.

Fourth, athletic leaders want their companies to win championships as well as single matches. Uncharacteristically for Russian CEOs, they make the long-term success of their organizations a very important element of their leadership agendas. Gref says, 'You can't think only three or five years ahead. Sberbank today is one of the most technologically advanced and efficient banks, but in ten years from now – it is non-competitive.'[4] This is why the Sberbank CEO has invested tens of billions of dollars in information technology (IT) (which he has completely reorganized three times in five years), hired several thousand software developers, acquired a handful of digital start-ups and built a corporate university for 36,000 people. Saveliev's agenda at Aeroflot includes projects that target 2025 – the year when he will be 72 and most likely doing something else –, yet he invests his full energy and passion in launching and monitoring them.

Lastly, all the athletic leaders we studied are patriotic and dedicated to making their country a better place. Some are very open about it, others less so, but they all care and, as we will see, use their leadership energy and the resources they control to further the cause of 'making Russia great again'.

Our protagonists are competitive individuals focused on winning. At the same time, they are leaders – people who are creating a new reality with the help of thousands of other people. Leadership is always about transformation, and this priority sits high on our protagonists' agendas – with a significance that is independent of business or personal achievement. *Transformation*, or positive change for its own sake, has a profound meaning for

---

[4] M. Ivanyushchenkova, 'Herman Gref: "Russian Management Style Is Not Efficient, But Effective"', *Harvard Business Review Russia*, 26 January 2016.

them. And, as with 'winning', athletic leaders pursue different kinds of transformation at different levels.

The most visible is *organizational transformation*. Athletic leaders change the way their companies operate and how the latter are perceived by the outside world. One of Saveliev's proudest achievements is the 180-degree change in the public perception of Aeroflot. During his first nine months as the company's CEO, the highly sociable Saveliev had to avoid public functions to protect himself from the inevitable barrage of complaints from other guests. He remembers those humiliating times well and is still working on improving his company. Under Gref, Sberbank has undergone a profound transformation, which has reached all elements of the organization – from corporate values to the company logo. No employee, department or process was spared from change, but what is most remarkable is that the pace of change has not slowed with time. Instead, it has intensified to an extraordinary level. The CEO wants to transition from a traditional bank, which grew out of the state savings organization, to a multiproduct digital company, providing a wide range of services – from banking to telecommunications to shopping – for hundreds of millions of people. Meanwhile at Gazprom Neft, one executive said that her CEO 'initiates organizational change for the sake of change itself, because he gets bored'.[5] Whether this is true or not, our research shows that organizational transformations launched by athletic leaders have had a positive impact on the performance of their companies.

Not content with organizational change, athletic leaders work hard to *change other people*, transforming their beliefs, attitudes and skills. They want to go beyond compliance and execution to full enthusiasm and commitment – and they do not limit this ambition to employees; rather, they extend their transformative reach to customers, suppliers and competitors, and sometimes even to top government officials. One of Kaspersky's employees describes his CEO in this way: 'Kaspersky's major role is to [...] establish standards for other employees. He aims very high, and he expects every employee to have an ambition. He works hard and he expects everyone to work hard. He learns and he expects

[5] In interview with authors.

everyone to learn. He does not care about form but substance – and he expects others to do the same. He instils his norms by walking around, talking to people and working with them.'[6]

Because of the passion with which athletic leaders try to influence others, some observers compare them to evangelists. Saveliev is philosophical about it: 'I don't care what they call me as long as they share my values – customer-centricity, innovation, superior performance and responsibility.'[7] Gref considers it one of his top priorities to advance the values of meritocracy, hard work and enlightenment with Sberbank employees and Russian people in general. With differing intensity, all our protagonists systematically invest in the development of human capital at their companies, and Gref has moved beyond that. Sberbank University trains customers, suppliers and even government officials, including the Russian prime minister and his cabinet.

On top of changing people's skills and attitudes, athletic leaders try *to transform their environment.* Dyukov says, 'The company has changed – it is a different company now in terms of volumes, scope, technologies, influence on the industry. We try to develop not just our company but the industry as well through legislation and initiatives for import substitution, helping the innovative community. This is its own kind of public service, our contribution to the country's development.'[8] The company has founded and supports a department at the St Petersburg Mining University. It has also launched the 'Hometown' programme – aimed at improving quality of life in the towns where Gazprom Neft is present through 350 projects in five key areas: urban development; the creation and development of sports initiatives for children and adults; education; development of the region's cultural potential; and, in the North, cooperation with indigenous populations. Gref promotes the concept of a productive business ecosystem: a network of independent players who interact, exchange, learn and do business with each other, with Sberbank positioned as the driving force. Kaspersky has become a global voice for cybersecurity.

[6] In interview with authors.
[7] In interview with authors.
[8] In interview with authors.

Lastly, but probably most importantly for understanding their leadership, athletic leaders are in the business of *self-transformation*. Some of them publicly state this as a top priority, while others do it quietly, but they all are engaged in a continuous project of self-development. Gref likes to repeat that he did not have the chance to receive a proper education in his early days, so he works hard to compensate for it through all available means – from lectures by Stanford professors to private coaching sessions. Saveliev's deputy at Aeroflot says that his boss has changed a great deal in recent years, in terms of both his knowledge and his style, which has become more visionary and mentoring. Their *mental toughness* does not always facilitate the self-development of athletic leaders, but their curiosity combined with their desire to evolve make it possible. This continuous personal transformation ensures that they stay up to date in an ever-changing world (Table 2.2).

Metapractices of Athletic Leaders

What makes leaders effective? There is a great deal of academic and practitioner literature that answers this question from a number of perspectives. The 'leadership style' school concentrates on the 'how?' question: how leaders interact with their followers. Different models have emerged in this area – from directive versus collaborative leadership to the Goleman-Boyatzis-McKee[9] model of six emotional leadership styles. Theories of leadership functions and roles following the early works of Max Weber and Chester Barnard describe 'what' effective leaders concentrate (or should concentrate) on, from setting direction to being a mentor for their followers.[10] Models of leadership competencies and capabilities occupy the middle ground: they define sets of specific behaviours (a combination of style and roles) that allow leaders to do their jobs.

---

[9] D. Goleman, R. Boyatzis and A. McKee, *Primal Leadership: Realizing the Power of Emotional Intelligence* (Boston: Harvard Business School, 2002).

[10] C. Barnard, *The Functions of The Executive* (Cambridge, MA: Harvard University Press, 1968); M. Weber, *The Theory of Social and Economic Organization* (New York: Free Press, 1964).

Table 2.2 Leadership Agenda: Self-Assessment

Please think about your own leadership agenda by answering the following questions. You do not need to have a formal leadership position, such as CEO or head of a business unit. Leadership is a process in which everyone can be engaged, regardless of position.

• What does your leadership agenda look like, that is, your plan to bring about change by improving performance and developing the organization and its people, including yourself? If you do not have such a plan, what might it look like? (See Table 2.1 if you need some inspiration.)

    ————————————————————————————

    ————————————————————————————

• Which areas does it cover? Do you have both performance and development/transformation goals? How clear are they? How ambitious are they?

    ————————————————————————————

    ————————————————————————————

    ————————————————————————————

    ————————————————————————————

• Does it have short-, medium-, and long-term goals? How balanced are they?

    ————————————————————————————

    ————————————————————————————

    ————————————————————————————

    ————————————————————————————

• Does your leadership agenda have specific projects that will ensure achievement of your goals? Does it contain metrics for success?

    ————————————————————————————

    ————————————————————————————

    ————————————————————————————

    ————————————————————————————

• What have you learned about yourself while completing this exercise?

    ————————————————————————————

    ————————————————————————————

    ————————————————————————————

    ————————————————————————————

We have chosen a different methodology to describe athletic leadership. Just as the quality and quantity of training and of competitive or recreation routines differentiate Olympic champions from other athletes, certain leadership practices distinguish athletic CEOs. Leadership practices are *specific, iterative, behaviour strategies for leading people and organizations.* We present five metapractices that group together the behavioural strategies of athletic leaders. Each allows a leader to deal with a specific metachallenge. We also describe some lower-level behavioural and mental practices and tools within each metapractice.

Pragmatic Exploration

Pragmatic exploration is a metapractice that allows athletic leaders to deal with the challenge of staying ahead of the game in an environment where products, technologies and business models are becoming obsolete with ever-increasing speed. Exploration is about continuously pushing the boundaries of personal and organizational expertise, expanding the frontiers of applied knowledge and striving for new discoveries. Just as great explorers of the past searched for unknown lands and seas, athletic leaders continuously look for new information, new ideas, new products and new ways of rearranging organizational resources. They have made learning and unlearning part of their daily routine, and, more importantly, they make exploration part of their companies' routine. Their exploration is total but pragmatic. They are not interested in amassing general knowledge; rather, they want to advance their organizations by acquiring or generating know-how that adds value. Athletic leaders explore when they are in the office, on holiday, at a business dinner or at a social function. It is non-stop work.

Athletic leaders have made *going out, going down and going deep* an important strategy of their pragmatic explorations. First, they continuously scan the environment: they *go out.* Benchmarking and market intelligence are the two routines that athletic leaders nurture in their organizations. Saveliev is very clear: 'I am not inventing a bicycle. I am looking for the best practice – and adopt it.'[11] Dyukov's Gazprom Neft has organized other oil companies to conduct comprehensive benchmarking exercises. Unlike many other executives who concentrate on their own businesses, athletic leaders keep their eyes wide open in search of best practices and new ideas that will enhance performance today and

---

[11] In interview with authors.

tomorrow – just like top athletes. They do not limit themselves to industry benchmarks but look for knowledge across the spectrum. We found that their companies spend heavily on global consulting companies such as McKinsey, BCG, Bain and the like. As Dyukov explained, 'We don't hire consultants for solutions, we hire them for knowledge acquisition. We will find solutions ourselves.'[12]

Although they derive learning from outside, our protagonists do not forget about their organizations and actively explore them at different levels: they *go down*. After earning a black belt in the Toyota Production System, Gref made Gemba (a practice whereby an executive takes on a front-line position for a day) a mandatory element of every Sberbank manager's job, including his own. He spends one day a month serving customers in various branches of the bank. Gref also regularly tours regional offices and speaks to customers, front-line employees and their supervisors. As his deputy Alexander Torbakhov says, 'Gref is in a constant dialogue with the bank. And this conversation is not so much about telling people what to do but learning from them about challenges and solutions.'[13]

As industry outsiders, athletic leaders defy sceptics by *going deep*. We were impressed during our interviews by how well they knew different aspects of their companies' business – from finance to technology – and how much they worked on deepening that knowledge. Oleg Bagrin, CEO of NLMK, explained, 'You can read as many books as you want, but there is only one way to learn about the industry: to walk about the (factory) floor. Initially the workers will try to overwhelm you with technical terms. If you withstand this test, they will see how relevant your questions are and how receptive you are to their answers. If they find it acceptable, they will open up and you will start learning amazing things that you could never learn from the most comprehensive report.'[14]

Athletic leaders do not lock themselves in an ivory tower at the head office; rather, they reach out to the lowest levels of the organization. They do so by walking around offices, plants and oilfields; servicing customers; immersing themselves in investment

[12] In interview with authors.
[13] In interview with authors.
[14] In interview with authors.

projects; and reading emails and suggestions from employees. The leaders we studied regularly 'go deep', spontaneously adding stress to the organization but receiving an enormous amount of first-hand data in the process.

The 360-degree search for knowledge creates a continuous inflow of ideas and insights for athletic leaders. Like the so-called '10X' companies described by Jim Collins and Morten Hansen in their book *Great by Choice*,[15] they do not spend months evaluating a project's pluses and minuses with formal analytical tools; instead, they perform rough calculations and *experiment.* However, unlike the 10X leaders, they go big – and even very big – with their tests. Athletic leaders seem to follow the combat sports wisdom: 'You will never know your real strength outside a ring.' Gazprom Neft's CEO made the overnight decision to change the structure of a multi-million-dollar acquisition, when new information about competitors' positions emerged. Gref, inspired by Frederic Laloux's book *Reinventing Organizations*,[16] created five experimental offices within Sberbank's Srednerussky Bank (based in the Moscow region) and later in Dalnevostochny (in the Far East region), which are working according to the philosophy of what Laloux calls 'Teal organizations'. These offices replace traditional managers with 'coaches', support the self-organization of their employees and focus totally on client satisfaction rather than financial results – following the motto 'acting here and now' for the client. According to Gref, it is too early to say how quickly and massively these practices will be implemented in Sberbank, but the initial results are already positive, in terms of both customers' satisfaction and employees' engagement and job satisfaction.

Our athletic leaders have demonstrated significant courage in launching large-scale pilot projects like low-cost airline Pobeda or the Prirazlomnoye Arctic underwater oilfield, but their speedy decisions are *data driven.* They have made a rational, fact-based approach part of the organizational cultures of their companies. They are fans of big data, real-time monitoring and reporting,

[15] J. C. Collins and M. T. Hansen, *Great by Choice: Uncertainty, Chaos, and Luck: Why Some Thrive Despite Them All* (New York: HarperCollins, 2011).
[16] F. Laloux, *Reinventing Organizations: A Guide to Creating Organizations Inspired by the Next Stage in Human Consciousness* (Millis, MA: Nelson Parker, 2014).

people analytics and so on. In less than three years Saveliev turned Aeroflot from a pre-Internet to a data-driven company. As we saw earlier, his 'Management Monitor' device provides 400-plus real-time indicators to the organization's key decision makers. It turns out that athletic leaders' pragmatic exploration is very modern – more like twenty-first-century science than fifteenth-century geographical adventures.

Exploration is a challenging journey that requires curious, open and well-prepared staff. Athletic leaders help these people emerge through their focus on *enlightenment and self-perfection*. Gref likes to say that he did not have the privilege of receiving a world-class education in his early years. He claims that he is working hard to catch up – and he is clearly encouraging Sberbank managers to do the same. Sberbank is investing hundreds of millions of dollars in employee education, ranging from language classes to MBA-like programmes with the top business schools London Business School (LBS) and INSEAD. It was Gref's idea to build the top-notch Sberbank Corporate University campus near Moscow, which now hosts 6,000 students every year. Gref's enlightening efforts do not stop at Sberbank. Not only does the Corporate University organize educational programmes for Russian government officials, including prime minister and his cabinet (as we have already mentioned), but Sberbank also sponsors a high school in Moscow, which has gained the reputation of being one of the most advanced in the country.

The personal development of athletic leaders is not limited to new knowledge acquisition. Like the ancient Greeks, they continuously work on training their intellect, emotions and physical endurance – striving for unity of mind, body and spirit. In one of his interviews Gref said that he has a six-point development plan for the year standing on his desk as a constant reminder. By practicing self-development and by actively promoting it, athletic leaders make it a corporate norm. Valery Katkalo, head of Sberbank Corporate University, confirms, 'if you don't learn constantly you don't feel comfortable at Sberbank'.[17]

---

[17] In interview with authors.

Navigating towards a Moving Target

While rapid knowledge obsolescence is a global trend that every business leader in the world has to deal with, turbulence creates additional specific challenges for athletic leaders. *Navigating towards a moving target* is a metapractice they have developed in response to extreme turbulence. It allows them to fulfil one of the universal leadership functions, which is to reduce the level of uncertainty about the present and future for followers, to map the road ahead, to allocate resources and to motivate and energize the troops. Under the traditional *Command-Control-Carrot-Stick* leadership model, this function has been achieved by setting long- and short-term goals, developing annual and five-year budgets and introducing long- and short-term management incentives. The traditional instruments remain, but for athletic leaders they take a back seat, giving room to some less orthodox approaches and tools.

Evolving – Yet Crystal Clear – Vision

Leadership vision – presenting a picture of the desired organizational future – has been praised by many scholars as one of the most powerful tools for managing knowledge workers. Athletic leaders actively use this instrument but with a distinctive twist. For them, vision is a continuous work in progress, one of the major tasks of any leader – based on ambition, experimentation and reflection. The company's vision evolves along with its business environment but has to be crystal clear at any given moment. This kind of vision provides the organization with direction, meaning and a benchmark for decision-making. In five years, Saveliev's vision for Aeroflot evolved from 'a customer-oriented company' to 'the most efficient European civic aviation group' via 'a service business' and 'a premium airline'. Yet at every point he was passionate about achieving the vision of the moment and relentlessly promoted it to the organization. Their natural adaptability allows athletic leaders to avoid one of the many traps that CEOs typically fall into: becoming stuck with an outdated vision.

Making Clothes with Room for Growth

There is an old joke (from a less politically correct era than our own) that when an Irish man stands in front of a high fence, he does not need to think about how to get over it. He just throws his hat to the other side and a solution will emerge. Unlike the 'Level Five' leaders described by Jim Collins in *Good to Great*,[18] athletic leaders do not follow the 'First Who ... Then What?' principle by involving staff in setting their own goals. Instead they set the bar at the 'world record level' and let their followers figure out how to get there. The initial reaction may be shock, but soon the followers accept the target, start thinking about achieving it and then go do it.

When in 2010 Dyukov presented Gazprom Neft's 2020 strategy, many executives dismissed it as 'surreal'. But the CEO remained firm and asked for plans to implement it. Senior managers started to think it over, ran a series of workshops and soon found it 'real'. Within three years the strategy had to be updated to raise certain targets.

At the same time, athletic leaders do not suffer from 'sunk cost' syndrome. They readily abandon programmes and goals that cannot be achieved or that have lost their relevance. Gazprom Neft dropped its ambition to acquire refineries in Western Europe when market conditions and economic sanctions made it very hard to achieve. Similarly, Sberbank revised its international expansion plans. Such moving of goalposts creates stress for followers. Yet the leaders themselves consider this practice natural and useful for growth and development. According to Dyukov, 'Stress is useful for a company as it is useful for an individual – a change in scenery. The need to work in new conditions helps develop skills and unite a team.'[19]

'Both Ends' Leadership

Alexander Torbakhov, Sberbank's head of retail, says, 'Gref constantly wants us to pursue mutually exclusive goals. For example, he

---

[18] J. C. Collins, *Good to Great: Why Some Companies Make The Leap ... and Others Don't* (New York: HarperBusiness, 2001).

[19] In interview with authors.

wants more innovation and more security at the same time or better service at a significantly lower cost. It blows many minds, but it works in the end.'[20] Athletic leaders defy the logic of traditional management dichotomies such as 'low cost versus differentiation', 'quality versus volume' and 'innovation versus discipline'. They want both at the same time and engage their organization in a two-directional pursuit of both ends of the spectrum.

Reinventing the Magic Solution

Athletic leaders help their followers deal with the turbulence and complexity of the environment by offering them ready-made mental frameworks and practical solutions. Often they borrow these instruments from other leaders, consultants or business school professors, but they present them to the organization with passion, vigour and the conviction that waving a 'magic wand' will make all the problems vanish. In due course, a new magic wand comes along and replaces the old one, but the goal has been achieved. The followers have received reassurance about the leader's – and their own – mastery over the turbulent environment. They have also learned a new tool and moved the organization forward.

Gref, the most dynamic 'magician' from among our protagonists, offers Sberbank a new framework several times a year. To date, the company has embraced 'learning organization', 'six sigma', 'corporate culture and values', 'emotional intelligence', 'Sberbank production system', 'big data', 'agility' and 'digital transformation'.

Slack Rope

We have borrowed the name of this metapractice – which athletic leaders use to deal with the challenge of managing their followers' performance and development – from world-class mountaineers. In the mountains, the most experienced person does not instruct other members of the team how to make the next move but always keeps an eye on the rope that connects them, intervening immediately in case of danger.

---

[20] In interview with authors.

Athletic leaders understand that it is not possible to build world-class organizations alone. They surround themselves with large groups of executives and extended leadership teams. Gref's management team at Sberbank consists of almost 250 people, while Dyukov invites 150 executives to the regular meetings of Gazprom Neft's 'extended management board'. However, the leader–team dynamics in these companies do not follow the popular recipes of inclusive and enabling leadership based on emotional intelligence. To pursue the sports analogy, our protagonists act as demanding captains of their teams rather than wise and attentive coaches. Their focus is on the game – the business – rather than on the people they are playing with. They set the goal and invite others to work together to achieve it. We have identified a number of specific practices and tools of *slack rope* performance management.

Do As I Do

It is hard to talk in the mountains. Less experienced climbers have to rely on observing their leaders' actions as the main way of deciding what to do. Athletic leaders are active players, and they manage their teams by setting high standards and living up to them. They work very hard and demand the same behaviour from others. They constantly learn and expect others to follow. They experiment and want others to try new things. They exercise and demonstrate phenomenal endurance – and assume others will work equally hard. Gref serves as an extreme example of this approach. He works 16 hours a day, reads 300 books a year, runs ten miles every morning and still finds time for charity and community work. According to Oleg Smirnov, head of Sberbank in Moscow, 'Working for Gref is like attending a top business school. This experience has made me a very different manager.'[21]

Dynamic Autonomy

Athletic leaders provide high degrees of autonomy for their followers but swiftly interfere when things go wrong. Saveliev describes his leadership as 'democratic-authoritarian': 'I manage

---

[21] In interview with authors.

by "variances". If I don't see negative deviation from the norm, I sit still. If something goes wrong I dive in.'[22] Kaspersky says that he pays a lot of attention to selection so that he can then leave people alone. But, as one of his managers told us, he controls all major processes in the organization and always 'keeps his finger on the company's pulse'.[23]

Encouraging Internal Competition

As highly competitive people, athletic leaders believe in the transforming power of competition and promote rivalry between organizational units and even the people who head them. Walking through Sberbank or Aeroflot offices, you see photographs of the 'employee of the month', the 'number one pilot', the 'best flight attendant' and so on. Sberbank's regional units are ranked on a quarterly basis, and their managers passionately await every new classification. One athletic leader told us, 'Our people are not very mature. Like kids, they need external stimuli to stay focused and perform. Competition is one of the best. That's why I am promoting it at all levels of the organization.'[24] Merciless to themselves, athletic leaders are not afraid to put extra pressure on followers, even at the risk of losing some of them.

Rewarding Loyalty and Performance

Athletic leaders expect their followers to share their ambition and to perform at the top level. In exchange they give generous awards. According to Kirill Kravchenko at Gazprom Neft, 'You understand that if the company performs well every three years, you'll receive a good bonus and you are ready to work hard in a three-year cycle, from the start to the finish.'[25]

Both results and attitudes count. Athletic leaders do not tolerate people with different values in their teams. Gref let go a few members of his team when he felt they became too complacent

---

[22] In interview with authors.
[23] In interview with authors.
[24] In interview with authors.
[25] In interview with authors.

or simply unfit. Saveliev changed his chief legal officers a few times, because they 'just did not see things the way we see them at Aeroflot'.[26]

Quiet Recognition. Tough Love

As we have just seen, athletic leaders do not hang on to their followers and let them go with ease. Contrary to popular theories of emotional intelligence and inspiring leadership, they can be quite severe with their teams, especially core executive teams. Our protagonists are great at challenging their team members but less skilful at supporting or mentoring them. Shamil Kurmashov, an Aeroflot vice president, explains, 'Saveliev is tough. He likes to say, "I am a composer – you are performers." '[27]

However, athletic leaders invite their executives on a unique journey, offer the opportunity to participate in building world-class organizations and provide ample resources for success. 'Dyukov is a restless person who demands a lot from himself and others. He rarely praises his subordinates, but never praises himself either. He delegates a lot, and you try to live up to that trust,'[28] explains Vadim Yakovlev. Athletic leaders recognize their team members by providing autonomy and resources and giving them challenging tasks, just like a football captain who passes the ball to effective teammates and gives them a chance to take a penalty kick.

Hogging the Limelight

The Russian leadership tradition puts any CEO in a tight spot. On the one hand, in a vertically organized society, the position comes with a lot of power. On the other hand, followers who deify their leaders expect miracles from them. If the magic fails to materialize, employees may not openly challenge the leader's authority but could lose interest and withdraw emotional support. This applies equally to external stakeholders. Athletic leaders recognize the challenge of constantly proving their leadership

[26] In interview with authors.
[27] In interview with authors.
[28] In interview with authors.

legitimacy and use the metapractice of *hogging the limelight* to overcome it. Like top athletes, they enjoy playing to full stadiums and like public attention and approval. Several specific behaviour and communication strategies support this metapractice.

Scoring Key Goals

As active, ambitious players, athletic leaders enjoy being in the middle of the action, calling the shots publicly and scoring key goals. Unlike 'Level Five' leaders, they constantly use the word 'I' rather than 'we' and do not shy away from attributing victories to personal decisions and actions.

Evangelism

Athletic leaders passionately promote their values, world views and specific methods and instruments to various audiences. Some limit themselves to their industries, while others, like Kaspersky, speak to the whole country or the whole world. To a large extent, it is thanks to Gref that the Russian business and government communities have discovered such concepts as productive corporate culture, lean technology, Gemba and agility. No other business leader we can think of has had a comparable impact. By spreading new ideas and models, athletic leaders create groups of like-minded people among their customers, suppliers, the general public and even regulators, which strengthens their ability to exercise leadership. One Russian executive shared with us this story: 'I transferred my accounts to Sberbank after I had listened to Gref's lecture on "run" and "change" as two distinct modes of organizing people and other resources. That was exactly what my company needed at that time.'[29]

Faces of the Industry

Our protagonists speak on behalf of their industries and set new standards for them. Saveliev of Aeroflot is an unofficial and influential spokesman for Russian civil aviation. He is engaged in

---

[29] In interview with authors.

a continuous dialogue with regulators to improve the market conditions and competitiveness of airlines. For years he fought to abolish article 108 of the Russian civil aviation code, which forbade the sale of non-returnable tickets. He finally prevailed in 2014, when the Russian parliament changed the code. Saveliev also led a successful campaign to allow the employment of foreign pilots in Russia.

Media Stars

The main protagonists of this book are among Russia's top CEOs for media appearances. They regularly give interviews to the business press and glossy magazines, speak on television and the radio and post their lectures and video clips online. Saveliev opens every issue of Aeroflot's in-flight magazine with a personal article (and a new photograph). Kaspersky has become a global media expert on cybersecurity and malware. The message to the public and to company employees is clear: 'We are present, we are active, and we keep winning.'

Chief Defenders

In their pragmatic explorations, athletic leaders proactively seek complaints and negative feedback from customers and employees as sources of learning and improvement. Both Gref and Saveliev cite Janelle Barlow's *A Complaint Is a Gift: Recovering Customer Loyalty When Things Go Wrong* as one of their favourite books.[30] Yet in the public domain they fiercely defend their companies and themselves, no matter how insubstantial the criticism.

On one occasion, Saveliev countered the not unreasonable criticism of Aeroflot's high fares with the following remark: 'OK, you don't like Aeroflot. It is expensive. You cannot afford it. But why give me a headache? Just fly with another company, go ahead. You pay Aeroflot for your safety and service.'[31]

---

[30] J. Barlow and C. Moller, *A Complaint Is a Gift: Recovering Customer Loyalty When Things Go Wrong* (San Francisco: Berrett-Koehler, 2009).

[31] E. Kuznetsova, 'Why Do We Need to Reduce Prices? Interview with Vitaly Saveliev', *Kommersant*, 24 April 2014.

There was a period when Kaspersky Anti-Virus was criticized for supposedly slowing down computers. However, Kaspersky's witty responses ended up all over the Internet and created a strong support group for both the CEO and his company. In 2007 when a journalist asked him if it was true that Kaspersky Anti-Virus slowed down computers, the CEO answered, 'It used to be true two technical directors ago. There was such a problem in a version released in 2000. Anyway, it was true, but this truth changed long ago.'[32]

Feeding and Milking

As we saw in Chapter 1, Russian government presents a formidable challenge to business leaders. Not only is it becoming more and more involved in business but also that involvement is ambiguous in many respects. The government regulates the economy but actively participates in it; it supports business but constrains its freedom. Government officials create and enforce universal rules for all economic actors but have private business interests in some of them. For some of our protagonists, the government also serves as a majority shareholder, and the Russian president as a key figure, who decided on their appointment. As one Russian CEO said, 'In my country government is everything – major opportunity, major threat, and major uncertainty.'[33]

To work with the government, athletic leaders have developed an equally ambivalent response, which we call *feeding and milking*. This metapractice has two facets. The first follows a rational logic of economics: in order to receive something, one needs to contribute. Both 'feed' and 'milk' have multiple forms, such as paying the correct corporate taxes, supporting specific projects, drafting legislation, attending important events or providing small favours to some officials (for the former) and receiving a greater level of autonomy, lucrative contracts or support for regional and international expansion (for the latter).

---

[32] A. Panasenko, 'Kaspersky Slows Down? It's a Myth!', *Anti-Malware.ru*, 21 March 2007.

[33] In interview with authors.

The second origin of this practice lies in the ancient Russian practice of 'feeding', whereby a nobleman received an estate from the tsar in order to oversee it, collect government taxes and extract a personal income. The 'feeding' arrangements did not take the form of a written or even an oral contract. It was a dynamic relationship, under which the balance of power constantly shifted between the principal and the agent. Both sides were interested in maintaining the relationship, but each had its own interests, which it was ready to advance at the expense of the other if at all possible.

Athletic leaders' interactions with the government are the most difficult element of their leadership practice to describe, as they do not like to talk much about this sensitive subject. Nevertheless, using secondary sources and interviews with some insiders who prefer to remain anonymous, we have identified some specific approaches that athletic leaders use to 'feed' and to 'milk'.

Working for the Country and for Their Communities

The protagonists of this book are patriots, who care about their motherland, wish it well and work actively to help it. Russia's well-being – as well as that of the regions where their companies operate – is an important element of their leadership agendas. It is one of the criteria they apply to the decision-making process and one of the informal lines of their investment budgets.

Displaying Loyalty Publicly, Challenging Privately

Athletic leaders demonstrate loyalty, respect and obedience in their relationships with senior government officials. They use expressions like 'I will report back', 'I will execute' and 'It will be done.' They play by the rules of a vertically organized Russian government. As Sergey Galitsky of Magnit puts it, 'I'm not going criticize the regime, I'm going to live in this country.'[34] And Saveliev says, 'I don't agree that government is an ineffective shareholder.

[34] I. Skrynnik and I. Prosvetov, 'Owner of Magnit, Sergey Galitsky: "I'm a businessman"', *Forbes Russia*, 15 April 2013.

A lot depends on management. There are some visible examples of effective state-owned companies.'[35]

Yet behind closed doors they fiercely defend their companies' interests in front of the most powerful politicians. When in 2015 the Russian government asked Aeroflot to save a defunct Transaero by acquiring it and assuming its debt, Saveliev firmly refused and negotiated a favourable deal for the company.

Athletic leaders do not limit challenging government to specific transactions that would put their companies at a disadvantage. They try to advance industry-wide issues and offer solutions to macroeconomic and fiscal policy problems. But this always happens behind closed doors and from the fundamental premise of 'supporting the government but challenging a specific idea'.

Proactive Contribution

Athletic leaders like to be in control even in their relationships with the government. They accept the fact that their companies have to make tangible contributions to important government projects, such as the Sochi Winter Olympics, the soccer World Cup or national health and education programmes, but like to choose the scale and form of the participation. They will listen attentively when the president, prime minister or a governor asks them for help, but they prefer to offer this before it has been solicited. As part of their pragmatic exploration, the leaders pay special attention to understanding the priorities of central and regional governments and the current agendas of their key government contacts so that they can offer them specific charitable projects, in-kind contributions and ideas for large-scale programmes.

Comprehensive Collaboration Rather Than Deal Making

Athletic leaders do not work with government officials according to the popular Russian expression 'Ty mne – ya tebe' (You will help me and I will help you). Rather they establish long-term relationships that benefit both sides and under which favours level

[35] M. Cherkasova, '"They Give You Nothing – You Don't Need to Pay It Back": Interview with V. Saveliev', *Kommersant*, 14 August 2012.

off over a period of time. They do not want to be seen as transactional, but at the same time they are not prepared to have a one-way relationship. When they feel the other side has pushed too far, athletic leaders counterattack intelligently but energetically – using a variety of instruments. They may refer to the interests of minority shareholders of their publicly listed companies, as Saveliev did in the Transaero case, appeal to other (competing) governmental bodies, leverage the media and general public or use the informal influence of powerful contacts. One senior government official describes his relationship with the CEOs of large Russian companies as a 'dynamic partnership'. 'We may have quarrels and serious ones, but we know that we need each other, and after a cooling-off period we continue to cooperate,'[36] he says.

Shielding the Company

Creating favourable working conditions for their organizations and teams is an important goal of athletic leaders. To achieve this goal they try to minimize government intervention in the company in all its forms – from tax inspections to appointments of relatives and friends to key positions. As one of them says, 'I work very actively with the government to allow my people to concentrate on the business.'[37]

Building and Maintaining Informal Networks

Like many other emerging economies, Russia is known as a country where 'institutions exist but connections work'. In this context, a social network of the right size and configuration represents a potential competitive advantage for anyone, especially a corporate CEO. Athletic leaders understand this and carefully assemble and maintain their networks. According to our estimates, each of them has an active network (at least one interaction per year) of two thousand-plus contacts, from the Russian president to heads of local administrations in remote Siberian towns, from the CEOs of FANG (Facebook, Amazon, Netflix, and Google) to front-line

---

[36] In interview with authors.
[37] In interview with authors.

supervisors, from Nobel laureates to aspiring authors. Athletic leaders value their networks immensely and manage them carefully. An executive who worked for years with one of them described the network management practices that he observed. He told us that the leader concerned classified all his contacts into four categories in accordance with their relative importance to him. He used contacts' birthdays as a relationship-maintenance tool, reaching out to all of them but using a different 'protocol' for each category. People from the least important received an SMS, while the second group was entitled to a phone call, the third a phone call *and* a present, and the most important an expensive present and a handwritten card. Each year the leader reviewed his network, shuffling people between different categories. Some names would be even removed from the list. Another executive told us that his former boss – another of the leaders from the study – calls him personally every year to say 'Happy Birthday' more than a decade after they had stopped working together.

Further Reading

Austin, R. D., Nolan, R. L. and O'Donnell S. *Harder Than I Thought: Adventures of a Twenty-First Century Leader.* Boston: Harvard Business Review Press, 2012.

Barnard, C. *The Functions of The Executive.* Cambridge, MA: Harvard University Press, 1968.

Bennis, W., and Spreitzer, G. M. *The Future of Leadership: Today's Top Leadership Thinkers Speak to Tomorrow's Leaders.* San Francisco: Jossey-Bass, 2001.

Brown, P., Roediger III, H. and McDaniel, M. *Make It Stick: The Science of Successful Learning.* Cambridge, MA: Belknap Press, 2014.

Conger, J. A. *The Practice of Leadership: Developing the Next Generation of Leaders* San Francisco: Jossey-Bass, 2007.

Galinsky, A., and Schweitzer, M. *Friend and Foe: When to Cooperate, When to Compete, and How to Succeed at Both.* New York: Random House, 2015.

Johansen, B. *Leaders Make the Future: Ten New Leadership Skills for an Uncertain World.* San Francisco: Berrett-Koehler, 2009.

Kaiser, K., Pich, M. and Schecter, I. A. *Becoming a Top Manager: Tools and Lessons in Transitioning to General Management.* San Francisco: Jossey-Bass, 2015.

Krames, J. A. *The Jack Welch Lexicon of Leadership.* New York: McGraw-Hill, 2002.

Mayo, A. J., Nohria, N. and Rennella, M. *Entrepreneurs, Managers, and Leaders: What the Airline Industry Can Teach Us about Leadership*. New York: Palgrave Macmillan, 2009.

Parks, S. D. *Leadership Can Be Taught: A Bold Approach for a Complex World*. Boston: Harvard Business School Press, 2005.

Pittampalli, A. *Persuadable: How Great Leaders Change Their Minds to Change the World*. New York: HarperBusiness, 2016.

Pink, D. H. *Drive: The Surprising Truth About What Motivates Us*. New York: Riverhead Books, 2009.

Reeves, M., and Harnoss, J. 'An Agenda for the Future of Global Business', *Harvard Business Review*, 27 February 2017,

Smith, W. K., Lewis, M. W. and Tushman, M. L. 'Both/And Leadership', *Harvard Business Review*, 1 May 2016.

Velsor, E. V., McCauley, C. D. and Ruderman, M. N. (eds). *The Center for Creative Leadership Handbook of Leadership Development*. San Francisco: Jossey-Bass, 2010.

Womack, J. P., and Jones, D. T. *Lean Thinking: Banish Waste and Create Wealth in Your Corporation*. New York: Free Press of Glencoe, 2003.

Films and Television Series

Aviator. Film directed by Martin Scorsese. Los Angeles: Appian Way, 2004.

Tucker: The Man and His Dream. Film directed by Francis Ford Coppola. San Francisco: Lucasfilm, 1988.

3

Effectiveness of Athletic Leadership: Outputs and Outcomes

I hated standing on that third-place podium. Hated it, hated it.
— Michael Phelps

My father says that if I hit 2,500 balls each day, I'll hit 17,500 balls each week, and at the end of one year I'll have hit nearly one million balls. He believes in math. Numbers, he says, don't lie. A child who hits one million balls each year will be unbeatable.

— Andre Agassi

Leadership is too complex a phenomenon to be measured easily. One very experienced CEO said that 'you cannot seriously talk about a particular leader's effectiveness until after ten years after her departure'.[1] Although we see the point, we cannot wait that long and would like to offer our view on the athletic leaders' effectiveness in this chapter.

For many decades leadership effectiveness was equated with the business results of the organization being led. If your company had gained market share and was more profitable than the industry average, you were doing great as a leader. Today this approach looks simplistic and one-dimensional. Organizational performance is influenced by many factors, and some of them are beyond the leader's control. Current results are to a large

---

[1] In interview with authors.

extent determined by past decisions, while the decisions a CEO makes today will have an impact on the company's results for years to come. We therefore need to add a time horizon when measuring the leader's impact on business results. We also have to differentiate between current performance (results that have been achieved) and contribution to future performance, that is, the creation of a platform for sustainable organizational development. It is important to note that sometimes current performance will reduce an organization's ability to win in the long run and vice versa. Effective leaders balance short- and long-term perspectives.

As early as the 1950s, Philip Selznik argued that, while business performance is a very important outcome of a leader's work, the primary function of leadership is to infuse purpose and meaning into the lives of individuals.[2] Since leadership is the process of achieving goals through the actions of other people, leaders – whether they like it or not – leave an impact on their followers. Leaders change how these people work, think and live, creating new meaning for them and (intentionally or not) teaching them new behaviours. The same applies to institutions and communities in which leaders operate or with which they interact. These changes or legacies constitute another very significant aspect of a leader's effectiveness.

One of our clients, the pharmaceutical company Teva, uses two terms to differentiate these two aspects of leadership effectiveness: outputs and outcomes. We refer to 'leadership outputs' when talking about business results, and we use the term 'leadership outcomes' to describe leaders' impact on followers, organizations and communities.

Outputs of Athletic Leadership

The most visible output of athletic leadership is a *stable, superior operational and financial performance.* The companies run by our protagonists consistently outperform the competition in operational as well as in financial metrics. The statistics in the following four paragraphs are nothing short of astonishing.

---

[2] P. Selznick, *Leadership in Administration* (Berkeley: University of California Press, 1957).

Since Vitaly Saveliev became Aeroflot's CEO, its revenue has more than doubled in dollar terms: from US$3.3 billion (106 billion roubles) in 2009 to US$7.4 billion (496 billion roubles) in 2016. Over the same period, net profit grew from US$86 million (2.7 billion roubles) to US$579 million (38.8 billion roubles), and the total dividends paid from US$12.1 million (388 million roubles) in dividends to US$288.8 million (19.4 billion roubles). Meanwhile, Aeroflot's market share of domestic flights increased from 17 per cent to 47 per cent, its share of international flights rose from 19 per cent to 39 per cent and the airline almost quadrupled its number of passengers from 11 to 43 million.

In AlexanderDyukov's case, between 2006 and 2016, Gazprom Neft reserves grew from 720 million to 1.6 billion tons, and annual hydrocarbons production rose from 46 to 86 million tons in oil equivalent, while refining increased from 24 to 42 million tons and sales of refined products from 24 to 40 million tons. Gazprom Neft's revenue has increased from US$20 billion (548 billion roubles) to more than US$23 billion (1,545 billion roubles) during Dyukov's reign – in spite of a significant drop in oil price. Currently, Gazprom Neft is the third-largest oil company in Russia (compared to being the eighth in 2007).

Sberbank has also demonstrated spectacular growth since Herman Gref became CEO. Sberbank's share of assets in the Russian financial market rose from 25 per cent in 2007 to 28.9 per cent in 2016. At the same time, loans to corporate clients almost tripled – from 4,900 to 13,633 billion roubles –, and loans to private clients rose from 677 to 5,032 billion roubles. Meanwhile, Sberbank's net profit increased from US$4.1 billion (106 billion roubles) to US$8 billion (542 billion roubles) in 2016. The net profit of Sberbank is currently 10 times higher than that of VTB Bank, the second-largest bank in Russia.

During the last decade Kaspersky Lab's unaudited revenue has increased almost 12 times in dollar terms and almost 30 times in roubles – from US$53 million (1.4 billion roubles) in 2006 to US$655 million (43.8 billion roubles) in 2016. Meanwhile its net profit reached US$89 million (5.9 billion roubles) compared to US$8 million (217 million roubles) net loss in 2006. The company sells its products in 200 countries and provides protection to over 400 million people and 270,000 corporate clients worldwide.

An even more remarkable output than the figures is our athletic leaders' creation of *solid platforms for future growth and development*. They want their companies to win in the long run, and they put together people, assets, products, technologies and processes that will ensure victory. Under Saveliev, Aeroflot created a portfolio of four brands catering to different market segments, made its fleet one of the youngest in the global industry, secured and protected profitable routes, built high brand awareness and achieved one of the best levels of customer service in Europe. With Dyukov at the helm, Gazprom Neft has mastered modern exploration and production technologies (including drilling and pumping crude in the Arctic), modernized its refineries and developed a cadre of competent engineers and managers. The future of all four companies looks promising, although we have to be cautious. History reveals many examples of firms with solid foundations that collapsed in a very short period of time – and often after a change in leadership.

Outcomes of Athletic Leadership

As we demonstrated in the previous chapter, winning is the number one item on the athletic leader's agenda. The second is transformation. And profound transformations of different types and sizes are among the major outcomes in each of our four main stories of athletic leadership.

Reformed Followers

Over the last few years, we have had the privilege of teaching in the 'Sberbank-500' executive development programme at INSEAD. This programme was initiated by Gref for middle managers with the potential to rise through the ranks of the organization. In its six years of existence the programme has been redesigned three times to reflect the speed of change – in the participants themselves. In the early classes we worked on developing an understanding of basic business and management concepts, building a business vocabulary and learning how to think and act as a manager. For the 2016–17 participants, all this is so last year! They are looking for the latest thinking in areas such as digital transformation, agile management, big data, product design and 'teaming'.

Employee transformation has been especially remarkable at Aeroflot, (in)famous until recently for its poor service and arrogant personnel. In less than three years its stewardesses learned to smile, joke, make 'small talk' in at least two languages and deliver 'slow service'. Similarly, members of Aeroflot ground staff proactively help customers and solve their problems (rather than explaining that it is not the company's fault) – and all this with a smile! Because of its sheer scale, Sberbank took longer to change the service behaviour of its employees, but it did eventually succeed. From Kamchatka in the East to Kaliningrad in the West, Sberbank's staff changed from cold, indifferent, ignorant and even rude, to friendly, careful, knowledgeable and engaged.

As educators and executive coaches, we know how hard it is to change the behaviour of one single professional. Collectively, our protagonists have made sustainable modifications to the behaviour of hundreds of thousands of employees! Even more remarkably, unlike Moses, they did not need 40 years of wandering in the wilderness to change their people's minds. These transformations have affected different employees in different ways – from a complete overhaul of personal values for some Sberbank managers to adding 'discipline' as a core corporate value for Kasperky Lab software developers. But in all cases our athletic leaders have significantly advanced their followers in two dimensions: performance orientation (winning) and openness (exploration). Ekaterina Matskevich, ex-human resources (HR) director at Gazprom Neft, commented on the outcome of moving the company's headquarters to St Petersburg from Moscow: 'We felt that the move opened up our people, made them ready to embrace even more change.'[3] Similarly, Oleg Smirnov, head of Moscow Sberbank, said, 'In my younger years I thought I was very performance oriented. After working for Gref for a year, I realized how wrong I was. After six years I think I am a different person in this respect. My instinct is to aim higher and to search for more efficient ways of doing everything – from interacting with my PA to building branch offices.'[4]

[3] In interview with authors.
[4] In interview with authors.

And Dmitry Saprykin, CEO of Rossya Airline, an Aeroflot daughter company, who has a legal background, says that Saveliev's total dedication to performance made him a very different man – still obsessed with results but open to new ideas and ready to experiment and make mistakes.

This transformation is especially remarkable in the Russian cultural context, where performance orientation and open-mindedness have never been universal virtues. The traditional Russian mindset does not link success, achievement and extraordinary results with hard work, continuous learning and tenacity. Originally, it was 'luck' – in the form of golden fish that could grant any wish, magic bears, wolves and birds, wise men and brave knights – that helped simple people achieve extraordinary results. Years of communism, with its focus on equality and centralized distribution of goods and services, only reinforced this traditional attitude. Unsurprisingly, in his early days at Sberbank, Gref considered the 'weak work ethic of the bank's employees'[5] as his major leadership challenge. After living for centuries in harsh conditions – in areas full of dangerous swamps and forests, wild animals and aggressive neighbours – and suffering from regular invasions from the East and the West, Russians developed high levels of conservatism and suspicion of strangers. Many attempts at modernizing Russia, from Peter the Great to Yegor Gaidar's reforms of the 1990s, stumbled because of this feature of the national character. Dyukov recalls, 'Making experienced field engineers even look at what others do was an enormous challenge. They just said, "We know better, we have been doing it for 20 years." '[6]

How sustainable are the changes wrought by athletic leaders against the background of this strong cultural tradition? What happens if an athletic leader leaves the organization? Aeroflot vice president Vadim Zingman believes that the new mindset has taken deep root and a new *corporate culture* has emerged. The leader's obsession with performance and openness and, in Aeroflot's case, with customer orientation has become a cultural norm independent of the role model's presence, which brings

---

[5] In interview with authors.
[6] In interview with authors.

us to the second important outcome of the athletic leaders' work: organizational transformation.

Athletic Companies

A friend of ours who lives in the United States returned to Russia a few years ago after ten years' absence. After walking into a Sberbank branch in Moscow and spending 20 minutes looking around in awe, he asked to go to another one to check that the first was not a fake – so dramatic was the difference from the Sberbank he remembered. Whether you visit the Kaspersky Lab head office in the north-west of Moscow or Sberbank's branch in the Siberian city of Surgut, you feel that you are on the premises of a twenty-first-century enterprise. Appearances can of course be superficial, but not to the athletic leaders, who believe that an office environment has a direct impact on employees' mindset and therefore on their performance. 'When people enter our office we want them to feel warmer, because it's dark and cloudy outside for almost nine months a year,'[7] says Natalia Germanova, Sberbank's marketing executive.

Our four main characters have also created new organizational architectures, which – allowing for the differences between a 250,000-strong bank and a software developer with just 3,000 employees – have some common features. These, we believe, help make the companies as strong and competitive as their leaders.

First of all, these companies are *fit* like world-class athletes. They have strong balance sheets, world-class assets and deliver sustainable performance (for details, see 'Outputs of Athletic Leaders' above).

These companies are also *united yet decentralized.* Saveliev and Dyukov started their organization building by 'collecting the company from semi-independent pieces' and wresting control from powerful regional and functional bosses, while Kaspersky first expanded his organization from a tight nucleus in Moscow into an international network. Yet both have ended up with a similar structure: a strong centre headed by a strong leader and autonomous units with direct links to the boss. Organizational unity

---

[7] Y. Chaikina, 'Sberbank: A Spate of Reforms', *Forbes*, 26 July 2010.

is reinforced by: a hyperactive, multipresent and superaccessible leader; shared ambition; some (in Sberbank's case many) core company-wide policies and procedures; effective (in many cases real-time) monitoring and control; and centralized resource-allocation mechanisms. Autonomy and diversity are achieved and preserved because of the tough-minded leaders appointed to run business units, the significant decision-making powers delegated to them, organizational complexity and even the geographical distance between the head office and operations. Vitaly Baranov, vice president of organizational development at Gazprom Neft, remembers, 'At INSEAD, when we had a case study about Napoleon and the Corps d'Armée system he invented, I said to myself, "Gee, this is like us – visionary leader in the centre, autonomous businessmen in the field, shared goals to beat the others in the industry, and intensive communication back and forth." '[8]

The combination of unity and autonomy makes these companies *robust and flexible* at the same time. In 2015–16, Aeroflot withstood two unexpected formidable blows: the halving of the rouble's value against the dollar and a 10 per cent contraction of the domestic passenger market. Yet the company's revenue went up by 19.4 per cent and the number of passengers increased by 10 per cent. At the same time (after an initial failed attempt because of Western sanctions), Aeroflot launched a low-cost airline, Pobeda, which became an overwhelming success – flying almost five million passengers in its third year of existence, achieving average aircraft turnaround of 25 minutes and reaching 93 per cent capacity utilization. At the same time the company added 26 new routes to its portfolio, fully automated its key business processes and introduced digital monitors for senior executives, pilots and flight attendants. During the same period both Sberbank and Gazprom Neft posted record financial results and launched multi-billion-dollar high-tech projects.

Athletic leaders have made their organizations *open to the outside world.* These companies may not be totally global in terms of geographical operation or management-team composition, but they are active members of the global business community. We watched the leaders permanently interacting with both domestic

[8] In interview with authors.

and global counterparts – exchanging, learning and collaborating. The same happens at other organizational levels. The companies we studied actively form alliances, partnerships and joint ventures with Russian and international businesses, including competitors, customers and vendors, and financial, consulting and research institutions. They actively participate in national and global associations and constantly integrate the knowledge thus acquired into their operations. They are significantly more active than other Russian companies outside the home market through foreign direct investments, joint ventures and other entrepreneurial formats. From day one, Kaspersky had an ambition to create a leading international antivirus company. And Kaspersky Lab started to export during the first year of its existence. The company made its first (failed) attempt to establish international operations only three years after incorporation. In year five it finally succeeded, and international expansion has been the major source of growth ever since. Today Kaspersky Lab has operations in Russia, EEMEA (Eastern Europe, the Middle East and Africa), Western Europe, the Americas and the Asia-Pacific – with offices in 32 countries such as Japan, South Korea, Great Britain, China, Germany, the Netherlands, Romania, Canada, UAE (United Arab Emirates), Kazakhstan, Uzbekistan and many others. Kaspersky Lab derives more than 70 per cent of its revenues from international operations. According to the former president of Kaspersky Lab Americas, the key to its success was in 'localability', the ability to acquire local knowledge quickly and to adapt to the local culture in each territory.

'Learning organization' may sound commonplace these days, but our experience in Russia and other emerging markets shows that organization-wide systemic knowledge acquisition remains a huge challenge for most companies. Our principal athletic leaders have created three conditions that have turned their firms into *learning organizations*. They have established learning, development and self-improvement as core corporate norms. As Nikolay Tsekhomsky, ex-CFO of Sberbank, put it, 'If you don't learn, you don't belong here.'[9] These leaders have made Peter Drucker's concept of 'protected budget for development' (no matter how

---

[9] In interview with authors.

bad the market situation, keep investing in learning and development) a corporate policy and put millions and millions of dollars into it. To ensure returns on this investment they have created modern platforms for organizational learning, such as corporate universities, virtual schools, company-wide mentoring, applied research centres and labs, and departments at universities and colleges. Not surprisingly, two of the organizations we studied – Sberbank and Aeroflot – compete for the title of 'the most digital' large company in Russia.

In the early 2000s Aeroflot had serious problems recruiting for the whole range of jobs – from pilots to cleaners; however, today it is one of the most sought-after employers. Athletic leaders share a popular view that 'talent is the major asset' for business in the twenty-first century and have energetically turned their companies into *hubs for mature – as well as aspiring – talent.* According to Ella Sytnik, managing partner of a leading executive search company, Ward Howell, 'If you want to be in the oil business and remain globally competitive in Russia, you have only one option – Gazprom Neft.'[10] It is indicative that, within the three years after TNK-BP (the joint venture between BP and private Russian investors, renowned for the quality of its management and engineering talent) was acquired by Rosneft, according to Sytnik, almost 'everybody who was anybody there ended up at Gazprom Neft.'[11] Likewise, there are more than five applicants for every opening at Aeroflot's school for flight attendants, and 800 foreign pilots have to date applied for a job at the airline. Kaspersky says that he has 'the luxury of choosing from a large pool of Russian talent, despite the fact that these people could work anywhere in the world'.[12]

Employee surveys at the companies and our interviews with executive search consultants have consistently revealed specific features of athletically led companies that make them attractive places to work. First, there is the leader himself. 'Sberbank is Herman Gref,'[13] says Ella Sytnik. 'People want to work for Sberbank

---

[10] In interview with authors.
[11] In interview with authors.
[12] Dorofeev and Kostylyova, *Kaspersky's Principle*, p. 61.
[13] In interview with authors.

in order to work for Gref.' Second, there are the ambitious organizational projects. Ekaterina Matskevich, ex-HR director at Gazprom Neft, says, 'When we communicated our investment in Serbia [Gazprom Neft is a majority shareholder of NIS, the oil and gas major in the Balkans], we were inundated with résumés. The same happened when we started the Prirazlomnoe project in the Arctic.'[14] A software developer from Kaspersky Lab, who shared only his nickname, 'Kolyan', told us, 'At GReAT [Global Research and Analysis Team, a unit investigating cyberattacks and identifying ways to fight them], we do work very few people in the world could do. It's very cool.'[15] Third, there is the continuous transformation. Anton Belyakov, a Sberbank branch manager from Ekaterinburg, says, 'You are never bored here. Almost every day something new happens and you gotta be up for it.'[16] Last but not least, there are the learning and developmental opportunities – and potential for career advancement both within the company concerned and outside. Ella Sytnik says, 'Sberbank, Gazprom Neft, Aeroflot and Kaspersky Lab have become what we, executive search professionals, call "academies": organizations whose employees are in high demand on the market.'[17] To complete the picture we should mention that the younger generation highly appreciates the digital- and social-media-friendly faces of all four companies.

To summarize, athletic leaders create 'athletic companies' – superfit, highly competitive and dynamic, with a strong focus on performance and improvement, and open to the outside world as well as constantly learning and being admired by the public. Some of our interviewees added a '*self-improving*' dimension to the list. However, we believe that it would be too early to accord them this characteristic – so important for twenty-first-century business – and yet so rare. As we have already seen in previous chapters, athletic organizations are very dependent on the people who built them – athletic leaders. The real test of self-improvement will come when these leaders are no longer around.

---

[14] In interview with authors.
[15] In interview with authors.
[16] In interview with authors.
[17] In interview with authors.

Wide-reaching Impact

Reformed people and athletic organizations are primary outcomes of athletic leadership, yet – as their leadership agenda is not limited to the companies they run – the outcomes of their leadership reach far beyond their industries, communities and countries.

Athletic leaders directly and indirectly *change the industries* in which their companies operate by creating new products, setting new standards, inventing new business models and changing regulations. In 2004, Kaspersky Lab revolutionized the global antivirus software industry by introducing hourly updates for its products. Gazprom Neft permanently expanded the frontiers of the petroleum industry by successfully producing crude oil in the middle of the Barents Sea and using three nuclear icebreakers to transport its products through the Northern Sea Route (along the Russian Arctic coast). Saveliev made the Russian government change its civil aviation legislation to allow the hiring of foreign pilots, the selling of non-refundable tickets and separate charging for luggage – which kick-started the country's low-cost airline business. Like top sports stars, athletic leaders understand the existing rules very well – and win within those constraints – but they also work relentlessly to remove them in order to be able to expand their competitive arsenal.

The outcomes of athletic leaders' work also transcend their own business interests. As already mentioned, Gref has introduced the Russian business and government communities to many current management concepts and techniques, and tens of millions of Russian people to mobile and online banking. Gazprom Neft's joint venture in Serbia has demonstrated what contemporary professional management can achieve under very challenging conditions – and has set new standards for thousands of local business people and hundreds of companies. Kaspersky Lab products provide cyberprotection for over 400 million people in the world. Aeroflot's low-cost daughter, Pobeda, has made long-distance travel affordable to millions of Russian citizens with moderate incomes and boosted domestic tourism. Around 12 per cent of its passengers have taken their first air flight in life with Pobeda.

The Reverse Side of the Medal

The protagonists of this book deserve a gold medal for their leadership. However, just as every Olympic medal has its cost, so too do the impressive results of the athletic CEOs come with a price tag attached. The most visible not-so-pleasant outcome is a high rate of 'casualties'. To illustrate, in 2008 Sberbank's management board consisted of 24 executives. Only five of them (including Gref himself) remained in 2017. During Gref's reign, 19 people have left the management board, and 7 new members have joined. The average tenure on the board is only 3.8 years. As one of the former members told us, 'After four years I had to step down. It was exciting, but I could not cope with the pace.'[18] Those who stay feel exhausted and have little life outside work.

The case of Sberbank is the most striking, although other companies have had their executive casualties as well. Kaspersky Lab has had a significant high-profile exodus. In 2014, Nikolai Grebennikov, who had been rumoured to be a potential successor to Kaspersky, left the company with six other top managers.

Athletic leaders seem not to worry too much about losing talent and are not going to adjust their pace, as they believe it is essential for winning. They reason along the lines of 'I work very hard; they should do the same.'

It is not only at the very top of the organization that athletic leadership takes its toll. Many rank-and-file employees complain about fatigue, constant pressure and internal competition. In spite of the fact that athletic companies are considered to be employers of choice, employee turnover remains relatively high. These companies are not for everyone.

Focus on hard work is not the only element of athletic leadership which puts a strain on some followers' lives. The CEOs' low empathy makes some executives feel lonely and disfranchised at work. One of them shared her feelings: 'I adore my work, but I don't enjoy it. I have to concentrate 100 per cent of the time. I have no right to be weak, even for a second. Actually I don't have

---

[18] In interview with authors.

the right to be a woman – I have to show iron will and masculine stamina all the time.'[19]

Athletic leaders speak about their teams, but these teams are of a particular nature. They are groups of players, each of whom conducts an individual game to help the captain to score. The domineering figure of the leader who encourages internal competition – does not allow for intensive horizontal collaboration and mutual support among executives. One consultant who worked for years with two athletic companies from our research described them as 'empires consisting of highly autonomous fiefdoms that stay together because of the will of the emperor'.[20]

Our protagonists are not completely unaware of or blind to this issue. In one of his interviews, Gref shared that learning how to praise subordinates is one of his developmental priorities: 'I very rarely praise myself, because I have the personality of a perfectionist [...] My colleagues have noticed that I don't praise others often and communicated it to me in my annual 360 appraisal.'[21] Yet it is not a natural element of their leadership style and will require significant mental and behavioural adjustments to be made.

Risks and Limitations of Athletic Leadership

We have seen that athletic leadership delivers superior operational and financial results, and transforms people, companies and industries. But like every powerful tool it has its own limitations and risks. Athletic CEOs do not like to 'waste time' on discussing them, and they press ahead with their leadership agendas, but we will pause and spend some time describing the most important.

The leader represents the major risk for an organization that is *overly dependent* on his or her ideas, energy, drive and social connections. If the CEO steps down, the company will have a hard time adjusting. This risk is augmented by athletic leaders' natural refusal to take succession and crisis planning seriously. Because they are performance and change oriented, they move forward without thinking much about unpleasant eventualities. Succession

[19] In interview with authors.
[20] In interview with authors.
[21] Herman Gref's open interview with users of VKontakte, 6 July 2016.

is a very challenging matter for all CEOs, but for athletic leaders, who eat, sleep and breathe their work, it is a double challenge. For them, succession is a sort of 'social death', and even thoughts about it create negative associations. As Sergey Galitsky explained in an interview, 'There is no successor issue. I'm not interested in what will happen after me. Why should I be interested?'[22] The athletic leader's prominence in the organization makes it difficult for other people, such as board members and senior executives, to step in and to raise the issue of succession planning. So athletic organizations remain vulnerable to their leaders' fate.

The high level of concentration of leadership in the hands of an athletic CEO creates another organizational risk in the specific area of leadership development. Although they value development and make it one of the organizational priorities, they do not take on the role of 'chief mentors'. Despite their preoccupation with personal and organizational performance, athletic leaders have little interest and skill in nurturing *other* leaders. They do not provide detailed developmental feedback, review challenging cases with subordinates, create developmental assignments or invite future leaders to share concerns and seek advice. The fact that none of our main protagonists has ever had a mentor does not help the situation. A company culture with a cult of performance and innovation also makes leadership development a challenge, since aspiring leaders have to deliver superior results and compete for the CEO's attention and approval on a daily basis, rather than experiment with new behaviours, ideas and approaches. We know that leaders develop by doing diverse leadership work, making mistakes, reflecting on their experiences and learning from other leaders. These conditions cannot be easily met in athletic organizations.

At the same time, internal competition can become a serious barrier to horizontal collaboration and effective teaming between different organizational units and levels. It may lead to such unhealthy and costly practices as the withholding and distorting of information, window dressing, rat races, political infighting and bad-mouthing.

---

[22] I. Skrynnik and I. Prosvetov, (2013), 'Owner of Magnit, Sergey Galitsky: "I'm a Businessman"', *Forbes Russia*, 15 April 2013.

'Change fatigue' represents another potential risk. Employees of athletic organizations may become wary of the ever-increasing pace of transformation and pressure to do more – faster and better. It may lead to a mass exodus of people, apathy among those who stay, 'Italian' strikes and other acts of resistance. Customary patterns of interaction may be disrupted, organizational values questioned and even the leader's authority challenged. The company may plunge into a serious crisis with long-term consequences.

Fear of disappointing a beloved leader is another danger. On a number of occasions we observed how managers in athletic organizations panicked and preferred to stall rather than run the risk of upsetting a CEO with an additional question or unorthodox solution. As we know all too well from our research on human behaviour and our practice in consulting that fear and innovation are opposite poles. Where the former rules, the latter does not flourish.

Further Reading

Bass, B. M. *Leadership and Performance Beyond Expectations.* New York: Free Press, 1985.

Beer, M., Eisenstat, R. A., Foote, N., Fredberg, T. and Norgreen, F. *Higher Ambition: How Great Leaders Create Economic and Social Value.* Boston: Harvard Business Press, 2011.

Bennis, W. G., and Nanus, B. *Leaders: Strategies for Taking Charge.* New York: Harper & Row, 1985.

Cameron, K., and Lavine, M. *Making the Impossible Possible.* San Francisco: Berrett-Koehler Publishers, 2006.

Chester, B. *The Functions of the Executive.* Cambridge, MA: Harvard University Press, 1968,

Gulati, R., Mayo, A. and Nohria, N. *Management: An Integrated Approach,* 2nd ed. Boston: Cengage Learning, 2016.

Hannan, M. T. and Freeman, J. *Organizational Ecology.* Cambridge, MA: Harvard University Press, 1989.

Katz, D., and Kahn R. L. 'Leadership Practices in Relation to Productivity and Morale'. In *Group Dynamics,* edited by D. Cartwright and Z. Zander. Evanston, IL: Harper and Row, 1960, 554–570.

Khanna, T. 'Contextual Intelligence', *Harvard Business Review,* September 2014.

Khanna, T., and Palepu, K. G. *Winning in Emerging Markets: A Road Map for Strategy and Execution*. Boston: Harvard Business School Press, 2010.

Kilduff, M. and Krackhardt, D. *Interpersonal Networks in Organizations: Cognition, Personality, Dynamics, and Culture*. New York: Cambridge University Press, 2008.

Mayo, A. J., and Nohria, N. *In Their Time: The Greatest Business Leaders of the Twentieth Century*. Brighton Watertown, MA: Harvard Business Review Press.

Mukunda, G. *Indispensable: When Leaders Really Matter*. Boston: Harvard Business Review Press, 2012.

Pfeffer, J. *Power: Why Some People Have It and Others Don't*. New York: Harper Business, 2010.

Podolny, J. M., Khurana, R. and Hill-Popper, M. 'Revisiting the Meaning of Leadership', *Research in Organizational Behavior* 26 (2005): 1–36.

Tedlow, R. S. *Denial: Why Business Leaders Fail to Look Facts in the Face-and What to Do about It*. London: Portfolio, 2010.

Wasserman, N., Anand, B. and Nohria, N. 'When Does Leadership Matter? A Contingent Opportunities View of CEO Leadership'. In *Handbook of Leadership Theory and Practice*, edited by R. Khurana and N. Nohria. Boston: Harvard Business School Press, 2010: 27–63.

Films and Television Series

Peter the Great. Television series directed by Lawrence Shiller and Marvin J. Chomsky. New York: NBC Studios, 1986.

Steve Jobs. Film directed by Danny Boyle. Burbank, CA: Legendary Pictures, 2015.

4

Vitaly Saveliev: Passion and Innovation at the Old Airline

I have short goals – to get better every day, to help my teammates every day – but my only ultimate goal is to win an NBA championship. It's all that matters. I dream about it. I dream about it all the time, how it would look, how it would feel. It would be so amazing.

– LeBron James

I don't fold under pressure, great athletes perform better under pressure, so put pressure on me.

– Floyd Mayweather

In the spring of 2014, Vitaly Saveliev signed his second five-year contract as CEO of Aeroflot, Russia's flag carrier. In the fall of that year a crisis struck Russia. Following a collapse in oil prices, the rouble lost almost 50 per cent of its value, Russia's Central Bank raised its benchmark one-week repo rate from 10.5 per cent to 17 per cent, and the fourth-largest Russian airline (Utair) defaulted on its bonds – all in a matter of weeks. Continuing Western economic sanctions added a few dark brushstrokes to an already bleak picture.

'Bad luck?' asked the 60-year-old executive who, in the previous five years, had turned Aeroflot from the 'airline to avoid' into a rising star of the European aviation industry, increasing yearly revenues from under US$3.3 billion to almost US$9.1 billion and net income from US$86 to US$230 million, lifting passenger figures from 11.1 to 31.4 million and improving labour productivity by a factor of 3 (see Table 4.1). 'Opportunity!' answered the seasoned leader, who had managed through many crises in his 30-year career. And he turned out to be right.

In the two years that followed, Aeroflot improved its market share and profitability – and strengthened its position as one of the most dynamic airlines in the world. Under Saveliev's leadership Aeroflot did what most businesses refuse even to attempt – reduced costs and raised the top line. In the fall of 2014, Aeroflot quickly adapted its strategy to the new economic reality by withdrawing seven planes from action, delaying the delivery of new aircraft, cutting administrative expenses and letting staff go. In 2015, Saveliev categorically refused the Russian government's request to acquire a defunct Transaero, the second-largest Russian carrier, for 260 billion roubles (US$4.5 billion) – but negotiated a deal. Aeroflot would fulfil all of Transaero's obligations to passengers in exchange for 56 of the failing airline's 97 routes. Over three months Aeroflot flew more than two million Transaero passengers across Russia and abroad and secured the routes for itself. The 2016 financial results turned out to be the strongest in Aeroflot's post-Soviet history.

Humble Beginnings and Ambitious Goals

The young Saveliev did not dream about a career at the head of a flag-carrying company. He had a more practical vision – to become the minister of construction of the USSR! It was not a boyish fantasy but the well-calculated plan of a rational person. Saveliev grew up in the Central Asian Soviet republic of Uzbekistan with his geologist single mother and housewife grandmother. The family lived modestly and, from an early age, Vitaly was determined to have a successful career. At that time he defined it as 'having an interesting job, an apartment and a decent salary'.[1]

After high school, he entered the elite St Petersburg Polytechnic Institute, which would have a strong impact on him and his leadership style. At university the career reflection process continued. Vitaly read books and listened to experienced people.

[1] In interview with authors.

One book by Alexander Yakovlev, a renowned Soviet aircraft designer and later a government minister, had a strong impact on him. The decision to become a minister was confirmed.

Saveliev went on to read more books and talk to more people in order to map a path to his target position – and concluded he would need to climb 14 steps. Today, Saveliev half-jokingly says that he fell 'one step short of his target': between 2004 and 2007 he was deputy minister of economic development and trade.

Sport played – and continues to play – an important role in Saveliev's life and leadership. During his childhood he practiced wrestling, but at the age of 17 he became a boxer by accident. Dreaming of learning to swim (now one of his regular workouts), he signed up for the swimming club at university but was sent away after the first class. The coach was looking for experienced athletes, not beginners. The only remaining option was boxing. He ultimately became the university boxing champion and won a national student tournament. With some self-deprecation he explains, 'I had a natural advantage – light bones. So I was taller than other guys in my category, but boxing taught me to concentrate and to work out regularly.'[2] Nowadays Saveliev plays tennis, works out in the gym and swims. He even puts his exercise videos on Instagram to show that Aeroflot's CEO is in good shape.

Saveliev's first job was a far cry from the glamour of the minister's office. A university professor had introduced Saveliev to a man who was recruiting 'young engineers looking for exciting work and a decent salary' – and who offered him a position in Siberia. Saveliev still remembers the first week on the job. He had to live in a tent in the middle of nowhere, surrounded by strange people, and was pretty much left to his own devices. The temptation to run back to civilization was strong, but Saveliev persevered and, after a month, 'started to like some elements of it.'[3]

He stayed in Siberia for seven years and, before turning 30, was appointed deputy CEO of one of the largest construction companies in the USSR. The experience profoundly marked the future business leader: 'I worked very hard, and at the age of 30,

[2] In interview with authors.
[3] In interview with authors.

I spent a week in hospital with work-related stress. There I began to reflect on my management style and to read management books.'[4]

In the 1990s Saveliev was in turn an entrepreneur, a senior executive in the energy and banking industries and on the board of a number of prominent Russian companies. But another experience that, he believes, shaped him as a business leader came from a government job. When Gref, currently CEO of Sberbank, became minister of economic development, he removed sixteen of his deputies and kept only two, one of them Saveliev. According to Saveliev, Gref had – and still has – a very strong influence on how he thinks and acts as a businessman. Their cooperation at the Ministry changed the deputy's perspective on what it is possible to achieve, even in a very conservative environment. While Gref continues to share ideas, books and videos with him, their old cooperation seems to have acquired some elements of competition, as is evident when Saveliev talks about Aeroflot's digitalization programme, comparing it rather favourably with Sberbank's.

While working for the government Saveliev met and built relationships with many prominent and well-connected people, forming a valuable social network that helps him, as Aeroflot's CEO, navigate ultracomplex relationships with a sphinxlike Russian government that happens to be the company's controlling shareholder, regulator and important customer all at once. According to Kirill Androsov, chair of Aeroflot's board of directors and an ex-Kremlin insider himself, 'Saveliev's network makes him self-sufficient in the Russian *Sistema* (system of power). He can open any doors.'[5]

Vitaly Saveliev: Profile of a Leader

Saveliev is a well-rounded athletic leader, but when we spoke about him with Aeroflot board members, consultants, vendors and executives, they all emphasized his passion, ambition to win and developmental focus. These three elements form a core platform of his unique leadership and define his agenda and the tools to realize it.

---

[4] In interview with authors.
[5] In interview with authors.

Ambition

In 2009, when Saveliev became Aeroflot's CEO, his brief from the Russian government – the controlling shareholder – was very simple: 'Save the company from bankruptcy and put it firmly on its feet.'[6] Saveliev was not inspired by this goal – he strives to win, not to clean up a mess. As a newcomer to the industry he did not have a clear vision for the company, yet he already wanted to make it into a world-class organization. 'Why bother with modest goals? If you aim low, you risk hitting the ground,'[7] he says.

Soon Saveliev formulated some very ambitious numerical goals for 2020:

- top-20 world airlines
- top-5 European airline
- 67 million passengers
- US$1 billion operating profit
- 383 airliners
- 45 per cent market share in Russia.

Saveliev commented, 'I am not interested in celebrating old victories. I want to win new ones.'[8] By 2016 Aeroflot has already achieved three of its goals – made it to the top-20 in the world and the top-5 in Europe and reached the desired market share in Russia.

Saveliev's benchmarks are the leading international carriers, such as Singapore Airlines, Turkish Airlines and Ryanair, and he takes pleasure every time Aeroflot beats them in some element of the game. He is not a modest 'Level Five' leader, as described in Jim Collins' book *Good to Great*. Saveliev enjoys personally receiving the awards Aeroflot wins and telling the world about the company's successes.

Passion

Industry outsider Saveliev in no time became an air transport diehard after joining Aeroflot. People who have known him for a

---

[6] In interview with authors.
[7] In interview with authors.
[8] In interview with authors.

long time say that this has happened with every new job Saveliev has ever taken. His passion for the business and the company he heads translates into decisions and actions that some observers find extravagant, but he could not care less.

Saveliev has made quite a few unorthodox decisions at Aeroflot and has stood firmly by them. He fired 12 staff members who refused airplane access to passengers with home-printed boarding passes, when that service was first introduced. He replaced traditional Moldavian brandy with Chivas Whisky, and, on his daughter's advice, introduced Russian ice cream in business class. He lobbied the Russian government hard and fought the pilots' union to allow foreign nationals to fly in Russia. One of his most controversial decisions was to keep the Aeroflot name and logo (against the advice of experts inside and outside the company, who suggested that both had negative associations with the Soviet Union, communism and even the Gulag), insisting that the company should respect its roots. Today, the Aeroflot brand is valued at US$1.55 billion.

Developmental Focus

Saveliev is a curious person. He is interested in almost everything – from cars to music, from photography to sport, from digital technology to philosophy. Like other curious people, he reads books, watches videos and surfs the Web, but his focus is on acquiring knowledge that can be put into practical use to achieve his ambitions.

When Saveliev became Aeroflot's CEO in the spring of 2009, the company had only enough cash to operate for two weeks. A couple of weeks later he learned from two of his deputies – Shamil Kurmashov, Aeroflot's CFO, and Andrey Kalmykov, who had applied advanced analytical tools to different aspects of the company' operations – that the whole business model was unsustainable. Kurmashov recalls, 'When we looked at the company fleet from an economic point of view, the conclusion was straightforward: it should be kept on the ground.'[9]

---

[9] In interview with authors.

The situation required immediate action, and Saveliev decided to take 26 TU-154 airplanes out of service (due to fuel inefficiency) and centralized the treasury function, freezing all payments except salaries, taxes and interest on loans. Then he moved on to reducing headcount and other costs. In all, 2,500 people were let go, sparking a media frenzy.

Though busy cutting costs and optimizing Aeroflot's operations, Saveliev and his team made learning about the industry part of their routine. Every Saturday they spent four hours listening to strategy consultants from Bain & Company and McKinsey & Company. Then they applied their new knowledge to Aeroflot. According to Saveliev, a number of initiatives came out of these 'classes'. He recalls,

> We learned that newspapers and magazines have significant flight weight and cost us extra fuel, so we limited the choice and saved US$17 million a year. The same was true for fuel and water charges.[10]

Bain & Company became Saveliev's trusted advisers. Partner Yury Spektorov describes the experience: 'Saveliev is an amazing client – very demanding but very open to new ideas. But they have to be proven, not wishy-washy stuff.'[11]

Saveliev continues to learn about the industry and leadership from multiple sources – from fellow CEOs of international airlines to Aeroflot flight attendants, whom he interviews on every flight he takes. He has also made learning a key element of the new Aeroflot culture.

The same approach extends to his hobbies. Saveliev is an amateur photographer with more than 40,000 followers on Instagram. True to his innovative spirit, he has invented a method of combining different photographic modes into a single image, winning approval from a number of professional photographers.

Leading Turnaround

Aeroflot is one of the oldest carriers in the world. Founded in Soviet Russia in 1923 under the name Dobrolet, it was given a

---

[10] In interview with authors.
[11] In interview with authors.

new name and organization in 1932. At that time Aeroflot was the world's largest airline. In 1990, Aeroflot carried 139 million passengers – more than any other company in the world – and flew to 102 countries.

After the break-up of the Soviet Union, the newly independent states staked their claims to Aeroflot's branches. Its assets were divided into many smaller airlines, with Aeroflot keeping planes to support international traffic and a small share of domestic flights in the Russian Federation. The former monopoly gave way to a highly fragmented market – there were 413 carriers in the Russian Federation by 1994. But demand was falling – passengers in Russia declined from 86 million in 1990 to 22 million in 2000. With the country going through a severe economic crisis, air travel became prohibitively expensive for most Russians. Having lost more than 90 per cent of its fleet, Aeroflot was just one airline in the crowded Russian market.

The company was losing market share in Russia, its financial situation remained precarious and it was heavily dependent on trans-Siberian royalties – fees paid by international airlines to the Russian Federation for using its airspace, a practice adopted in the 1950s from which Aeroflot collected royalties. The global financial crisis of 2008–2009 hit Russia's aviation industry hard. Gross domestic product (GDP) contracted by 7.8 per cent and the passenger market saw double-digit decline. Aeroflot was losing passengers and bleeding cash. When Saveliev became CEO in April 2009, the company had enough money for two weeks of business.

The worldwide airline industry had gone through turbulent times at the beginning of the twenty-first century. At the time of Saveliev's appointment, passenger volume was just starting to rebound after the global financial crisis. Despite growth expectations in emerging markets, developed markets remained the key contributors to the global profit pool. The financial performance of the larger players was challenged, confirming the need for large-scale acquisitions (that took place mainly along alliance lines) and business model adaptation. Low-cost carriers (LCC) became the profit-margin leaders in North America and Europe, while the boundaries between incumbents and LCCs began to blur, further intensifying industry competition. Although mergers provided cost synergies and improved cost positions, they could not resolve the fundamental cost disadvantages facing many of the legacy carriers. Players kept upping the stakes to win customers, and it became harder to differentiate products and services.

The Saturday workshops with Bain & Company consultants confirmed what Saveliev knew from his own passenger experience: an airline is a service business. Soon after becoming CEO, he created the position of vice president for customer service, reporting directly to him. After stabilizing Aeroflot's financial situation, the management team focused on what they believed was critical for retaining existing passengers and attracting new ones: service quality. And they started with the 'face of the company', the flight attendants. Three aspects, according to Saveliev, had a tremendous impact on changing traditional perceptions of Aeroflot as a poor service airline: stewards' training, stewards' uniforms and in-flight food. Vadim Zingman, Aeroflot's vice president for customer service, who followed Saveliev from Sistema, added 'new marketing and PR strategies' to the list.

Trusting his own passenger experience ('I flew millions of miles with all major airlines as a customer.'[12]), Saveliev turned to Asian airlines in search of best practices in preparing flight attendants. With the help of Gref, he sent 60 carefully selected flight attendants to the Singapore Airlines training centre in charge of flight crew training. Twelve of them became the first coaches at Aeroflot's staff training centre in Moscow. As Saveliev explained,

> Our people simply did not know what service is all about. For example, they could not make 'small talk' with passengers; they felt it was not useful and distracted them from their work. The same was true about serving meals – our stewards rushed to deliver food, while Asians took time and let passengers enjoy it.[13]

Today, Aeroflot's training centre is among the largest in Europe. Future flight attendants study for 20 weeks and learn a variety of skills from 'slow service' to swimming in cold water and how to deliver a baby on-board.

---

[12] In interview with authors.
[13] In interview with authors.

Together with upgrading training, Aeroflot improved its hiring process. The company required all its future flight attendants to have a college degree, to speak English and to have good communication skills and emotional stability. They preferred to hire people without an airline background, since it was 'easier to learn than unlearn and learn again'[14] (as Androsov put it). All applicants had to go through psychometric and general intelligence tests.

Today, there are five candidates for every steward vacancy at Aeroflot. Anna, a flight attendant for two years, says, 'I work for Aeroflot because I love to visit new places, but I also like all the new things they teach us here. It's hard work, but it's very interesting.'[15]

Saveliev's second project was to dress up Aeroflot:

> When I looked at the issue, I had a headache – there were dozens of uniforms and people wore what they wanted. On the same flight with five stewards, each of them could wear a different uniform.[16]

In 2009, Aeroflot announced a tender for a new uniform design. All interested designers were invited to a meeting with Saveliev, who showed them a Virgin Atlantic video clip with the slogan '25 years. Still red hot.' He said, 'I want better than that' and left the room. He later acknowledged that his son had sent him the video in the first place, and that it had inspired him. Two Russian designers won the competition and produced a collection in 'red mandarin' (summer) and navy (winter). In early 2013, the Aeroflot uniform was voted the most stylish in Europe in a passenger survey.

Another important issue was food. Saveliev took the management team by surprise when he invited them to taste Aeroflot's food offerings. The effect was overwhelming – everyone admitted that the food was not acceptable:

> We had what I call 'a shot in the stomach' – overcooked beef with cheese and mayonnaise on top. It turned out that the senior

---

[14] In interview with authors.
[15] In interview with authors.
[16] In interview with authors.

steward decides what the menu is going to be and where to buy the food from. We centralized it and attracted top talent – chefs and sommeliers – to develop menus for Aeroflot.[17]

Today there are 16 set menus at Aeroflot (vegetarian, kosher, halal etc.), which change every three months in business class and twice a year in economy. The tradition of senior management tasting airline food remained, but Saveliev turned it into a show by inviting celebrities to participate. In 2015, Aeroflot took second place in the Skyscanner annual study of the quality of on-board menus in the long-haul dining category.

Given Aeroflot's poor image, especially abroad, executives had spent days and weeks debating what kind of marketing and advertising could help communicate the change. Said Zingman,

> We opted for brand ambassadors – well-known people who our potential customers trust. I cannot overstate the effectiveness of signing Manchester United as an Aeroflot partner. It had a strong impact on customer loyalty, especially in critically important Asian markets.[18]

When Saveliev joined Aeroflot he discovered that he had, in his own words, '29 deputies aged from 60 to 67 years'.[19] Aeroflot's senior executives mostly moved up through the ranks, and many of them had been pilots, navigators or technicians in the past. They loved and understood the technical side of the business, but their financial knowledge and managerial skills did not match Saveliev's expectations:

> They have done some great things in safety, pilot training, and technical support, but most of them didn't know financial terms like 'EBITDA' or 'cash flow'. At that time, Aeroflot management didn't even use email.[20]

But the new CEO did not rush to fire the old guard. He complemented the existing executive group with five managers

[17] In interview with authors.
[18] In interview with authors.
[19] In interview with authors.
[20] In interview with authors.

who had worked for him before and began to assess the potential of the old-timers. Some, such as Vladimir Antonov, who had joined Aeroflot 20 years earlier after a military career (now Saveliev's first deputy) and Igor Chalik, one of the first Russians to fly the Airbus (now in charge of Aeroflot flight operations), became key members of his team. The team met once a week as a group, and each member had a weekly tête-à-tête with the CEO. Saveliev describes his management style as 'democratic-authoritative':

> I always listen to people, I encourage them to speak their mind, but I make them learn that the final decision is mine and it's not up for discussion. I make it and I assume the risks that come with it.[21]

Building the Foundations of a Global Champion

By the end of 2010, Aeroflot had caught a new growth wave, regained market leadership in Russia from S7 Airlines, improved its financial position and was starting to get positive press. The initial executive actions had paid off, but the management team knew that most of the low-hanging fruit had been harvested and the company needed to define its longer-term strategy. The CEO was very clear about the ambition: to become the most profitable airline in the world and to be among the top largest European carriers. How to reach that goal? Saveliev did not know it then, but he had the team to work it out.

The work began in early 2011, with the participation of Bain & Company as strategic consultants. It was at that time that the first non-Russian executive, Giorgio Callegari, joined the Aeroflot management board as head of strategy. An industry veteran with a broad experience in sales, marketing, strategy and operations, he had previously worked for Alitalia. His arrival brought a new dynamic to the functioning of the management team – all meetings with his direct involvement were henceforth conducted in English. Six months later, Callegari requested that Russian be reinstated. He felt it was a Russian company and his Russian was now operational.

---

[21] In interview with authors.

In developing the new strategy, the Aeroflot management did a great deal of industry analysis and benchmarking. Saveliev insisted, 'I am not inventing a bicycle. I am looking for the best practice and adopt it.'[22] His core benchmarks were Turkish Airlines, Air France, British Airways and Lufthansa, but he also looked at the industry as a whole and beyond, as Androsov, Aeroflot chairman, confirmed:

> We took a hard look at the industry and we realized that traditional airlines – British Airways or Air France – will not survive. Low-cost airlines will kill them. In the future you can be either a low-cost or a premium airline.[23]

Aeroflot decided to be a premium carrier. To become a premium airline, first and foremost it had to provide premium service. For that, it had to assure safety, great planes, friendly on-board service and seamless support on the ground. Providing a great safety experience meant Aeroflot had to focus on upgrading its fleet and customer service, and doing so in a profitable way. Russia's geographic position provided a unique market opportunity – to link Europe with the emerging economies of East Asia, which also became a part of the new strategy.

Aeroflot made a significant investment in its fleet, acquiring new Airbuses, Boeings and Sukhoi Superjets, and becoming one of the youngest fleets in the world, with an average age of 4.2 years (for comparison, the average at Lufthansa Group is 11.3 years). Management did a great job at optimizing its acquisitions through diversification of suppliers and leasing, although some of these measures turned out to be excessive when the market dived in 2015.

The company built a modern terminal in Moscow Sheremetyevo airport to serve its Europe–Asia links and enjoyed high growth in this segment. According to Chairman Androsov, 'Passengers travelling from Europe to Asia and back became our best customers. These routes are very profitable both in business and economy class.'[24]

---

[22] In interview with authors.
[23] In interview with authors.
[24] In interview with authors.

Innovation was another element of the Aeroflot strategy. Management believed that a premium airline should surprise and delight its customers. Saveliev set an example with his constant search for innovation, scanning the world for ideas. He talked to friends, customers and experts, and read passengers' complaints on Twitter. One of his favourite books was called *A Complaint Is a Gift*. He recalls,

> We managed to insert new content into the old form. Aeroflot is one of the oldest airlines in the world, but we are a dynamic innovative company. We were first in Russia to have a working website, Wi-Fi, Internet et cetera.[25]

In the quest for innovation, he was not only a visionary who shows the way but also an active creator:

> I don't like it when people put their shoes on our blankets, but I can't prevent them from doing it, because passengers pay their money for the tickets. I ordered blanket dry-cleaning after each flight. It costs us millions of dollars, but customers love it.[26]

A lover of data, Saveliev turned Aeroflot into a data-driven company, creating dozens of indicators of where the company stands in customer service, customer loyalty, fleet efficiency, food quality and so on. Zingman, vice president for customer service, explains the sophisticated system of collecting and analysing critical data – customer satisfaction, customer complaints, operational statistics and competitor intelligence:

> In every department we have people responsible for innovation. Today innovative ideas mostly come from these people and systemic solutions. The days of low-hanging fruit, when Saveliev or other senior executives could come up with a brilliant idea based on common sense, are gone.[27]

His employees flew competitors' flights a few times every month and submitted comprehensive reports. Customer surveys provided unexpected insights. In 2010, Aeroflot learned that its

---

[25] In interview with authors.
[26] In interview with authors.
[27] In interview with authors.

business-class customers considered quality of food, entertainment and attractiveness of flight attendants as the three most important differentiators (an industry-wide assumption was that business passengers cared more about timing, ease of access and availability of lounges). Following these findings, the company rethought its customer service priorities for business-class passengers.

Today, Aeroflot's 90 top executives are equipped with so-called 'executive monitors' – iPads providing access to 427 of its operational and financial indicators. In real time, they can find out which route is the most profitable, the occupancy rate of each flight, how many tickets have been sold through which channel, how productivity has changed and so on. Aeroflot pilots have their own tablets with the relevant data. Aeroflot is very serious about digitalization and has invested billions of roubles, making itself a truly digital company.

Innovation was not limited to services and products. The Aeroflot group, combining five airlines operating under separate brands, was created to provide customer segments that the premium parent company was unable or unwilling to serve. Its CEO constantly challenged the existing system of alliances that does not allow code-sharing between members of different alliances, and was determined to change the established rules. The company developed a project for a low-cost airline, which was created despite the obstacles the airline faced (the launch had to be delayed because of the EU sanctions). On top of that, Aeroflot invested 10 per cent of its annual profits in research and development (R&D).

According to Saveliev, Aeroflot had become a 'strategy-driven company', and it had paid off. It consistently won international awards for service quality and received positive international press reviews. Indeed, with a 'Net Promoter Score' of 72 per cent, it had the highest customer loyalty rating of any European airline.

Aeroflot had become an attractive employer not only for Russian but also for global talent. One recruitment effort to hire foreign pilots attracted more than 800 applications, although the company did not pay a premium compared to its European competitors.

The company continued to receive trans-Siberian royalties, but its profitability was no longer dependent on them. Androsov says,

> We are ready to live without royalties at any time. The CEO is more careful and is not rushing to renounce the money in favour of the Russian government. Relieve us from social obligations and we will give up the royalties.[28]

As a shrewd businessman, Saveliev understood that Aeroflot was more than a commercial airline. Rather, it is a national carrier in which the government owns the major stake. The company has actively participated in programmes to improve the lives of underprivileged Russian citizens. One of its daughter companies provides at-cost services to the extreme east, flying thousands of Second World War veterans to visit the former battlefields. Its charity programmes 'Heart with two wings' transport seriously ill children from remote locations for medical treatment in Moscow, and 'Train of Hope' flies prospective parents to Russia's orphanages. In 2013, more than 400 children received medical assistance in Moscow, and 100 orphans found new families. His network has helped persuade rich and famous Russians to support such initiatives, and there are plans to grow them further. Aeroflot has also helped Russian citizens caught in hotspots like Syria or Yemen by dispatching planes to bring compatriots home. Such actions impact the bottom line, but nobody questions them. They are intrinsic to the Aeroflot mission.

Saveliev's Leadership, Culture and Legacy

Saveliev believes in reflective leadership:

> I manage by 'variances.' If I don't see deviation from the norm, I sit still. If something goes wrong, I dive in. A general manager should create a team, allocate roles and let people work.[29]

Saveliev's deputies admire their CEO but acknowledge that working for him is not easy. The word they use most often to

---

[28] In interview with authors.
[29] In interview with authors.

describe their boss is 'tough'. As Dmitry Saprykin, vice president for sales and assets management, explains, 'He is a tough manager. Initially it was not easy to communicate, but I learned a lot from him.'[30] Shamil Kurmashov adds, 'Saveliev likes to say, "I am a composer – you are performers," But he is always concentrated, never late, loves structure and he delivers.'[31] The experienced Callegari is more philosophical: 'He is tough. But it's natural for an airline CEO.'[32] Dmitry Saprykin explains how Saveliev is a role model and an effective mentor for his managers:

> Saveliev is very effective and efficient and we learn it from him. For example, he always says that we should not spend more than one hour discussing a question – if we don't have a solution, let's take a pause and meet again – and I do the same. Being very performance oriented, Saveliev taught me not to be afraid of making mistakes. It sounds simple, but it is not trivial in our culture.[33]

Saveliev's role at Aeroflot has evolved over the last five years, as Saprykin – and colleagues – acknowledge:

> At the very beginning he centralized almost everything. I think that was also the way for him to understand the organization and to calibrate people. Since then we [VPs] have learned to solve operational problems and Saveliev can concentrate on higher levels.[34]

Zingman says,

> Saveliev controlled every detail, every order he gave. After he gained confidence in us, he moved to more strategic issues. He also works as the face of the company. We position him as an experienced manager, who is open to new ideas, a doer, and a customer adept. He does a great job communicating this image to multiple audiences.[35]

---

[30] In interview with authors.
[31] In interview with authors.
[32] In interview with authors.
[33] In interview with authors.
[34] In interview with authors.
[35] In interview with authors.

Kurmashov says,

> Nowadays Saveliev concentrates on government relations, works
> with other airlines and, of course, directly with customers.[36]

Saprykin says,

> In our collaboration with the CEO, we moved from a culture of
> executors of his ideas to the culture of generating those ideas. It's a
> big change.[37]

Cultural change rather than stunning financial results was what
Saveliev and his team are most proud of:

> When I joined Aeroflot, I could not attend social functions –
> people would jump on me with their criticism of the company. Five
> years later, I proudly listen to compliments from people of very
> different backgrounds and tastes.[38]

Zingman points to two major changes:

> Internally we made people realize that they need to work to earn
> their salary – work for the customer, not for themselves; we created
> a business culture. Externally we built a prestigious airline with
> which people want to associate themselves.[39]

Speaking about the future, Saveliev mentions the issue most CEOs
try to avoid: succession:

> I have two potential successors, both within the company, and
> I will work on developing them. But I know that it's not enough.
> I listened to a Boeing executive who said that they had a rule – to
> have two successors for today, another two for three years from now
> and another two for six years from now. That is solid.[40]

---

[36] In interview with authors.
[37] In interview with authors.
[38] In interview with authors.
[39] In interview with authors.
[40] In interview with authors.

Does he think about his retirement? 'No time for that.' He plays tennis every morning, travels the world and reads many books:

> A business leader needs to know what is written about business, but should not limit himself to reading business books. I learn a lot from classic and contemporary literature.[41]

In response to a final question about his legacy, he has no hesitation:

> I work to make sure the innovation spirit is preserved when I am gone and I find myself proudly flying Aeroflot.[42]

[41] In interview with authors.
[42] In interview with authors.

Table 4.1 Aeroflot Performance (2009–16)

	2009	2010	2011	2012	2013	2014	2015	2016
Financial indicators								
Revenue (RUB billion)	106.1	131.2	158.1	253.0	291.0	319.8	415.2	495.9
Revenue (USD million)	3,346	4,319	5,378	8,139	9,135	8,323	6,811	7,398
EBITDAR (RUB billion)	23.7	31.8	30.1	38.5	51.0	48.7	103.1	137.6
EBITDAR (USD million)	747	1,047	1,024	1,238	1,602	1,267	1,692	2,052
Net income (RUB billion)	2.7	7.7	14.4	5.2	7.3	(17.1)	(6.5)	38.8
Net income (USD million)	86	253	491	166	230	(446)	(107)	579
Operating indicators								
Passengers (million)	11.1	14.1	16.4	27.5	31.4	34.7	39.4	43.4
Load factor (%)	70.2%	77.1%	76.8%	78.1%	78.2%	77.8%	78.3%	81.4%
Fleet size	166	143	236	233	239	261	262	292
Number of employees (thousand)	19.1	20.5	28.4	28.8	30.5	32.2	34.0	36.6

Source: Aeroflot Annual Reports

5

Eugene Kaspersky: Saving the World

I am an expert at adaptation and overcoming adversity. We win or we learn, that's what my coach John says, and that's what we do.

— Conor McGregor

I love competition, so when you talk and tell me what you're gonna do, all it makes me wanna do is work harder.

— Usain Bolt

Eugene Kaspersky is an unconventional leader. When you enter Kaspersky Lab HQ you feel as if you have stepped out of Moscow straight into California. Employees wear colourful T-shirts, shorts and sandals. Sunshine floods through enormous windows into a vast open space. The CEO occupies a small glass-walled corner office filled with Kaspersky Lab memorabilia, while software programmers working on new endpoint protection products sit right next to his suite. The message is clear: these guys are the most valuable resource of the company. 'And they are fun to talk with,'[1] confides Kaspersky.

Dressed in a green Hawaiian shirt ('We are a green company'), jeans and sneakers, and talking fast in heavily accented English, Kaspersky looks more like a programming genius than the CEO of a global company. 'I don't give a damn about how I am dressed. I have a cheap watch and I adore jeans. I only care about comfort,'[2]

[1] In interview with authors.
[2] V. Dorofeev and T. Kostylyova, *Kaspersky's Principle: Internet Bodyguard* (Moscow: Eksmo, 2011), p. 126.

he says. With unbridled passion, Kaspersky explains that the world is full of bad guys of different types – hackers, thieves, organized crime, rogue businesses and governments. They are becoming more and more sophisticated in the ways they conduct their dirty business, and their negative impact on the global economy is becoming more and more tangible. It is not possible to eradicate them altogether, but his mission is to make their lives very tough indeed – and he is confident he knows how to do it. Kaspersky Lab is engaged in developing and distributing antivirus protection software, which creates positive cash flows. However, the company also assists national governments and international security bodies (such as Europol and Interpol), actively participating in joint investigations of cyberespionage or cybersabotage malware and providing technical expertise. These activities require cash disbursements but give the founder even more moral satisfaction than his highly profitable products.

Kaspersky Lab is, according to him, a company driven by talent and values: 'I realized a long time ago that in order to make serious money, one should never think about making money but about doing something well. The money will come.'[3] How this eccentric, former-Soviet programmer managed to build not only a sizeable and profitable business but also a global company remains a mystery for many observers. However, a closer look at Kaspersky Lab's story and Eugene Kaspersky's leadership provides a full explanation.

History

The story of Kaspersky Lab began in 1989, when a young fellow at a closed scientific research institute detected a virus on his desktop computer. Kaspersky tried to cure his machine – and succeeded. In the next two years, in addition to working at the institute, the young researcher continued to play with viruses and malware. Defeating them became not just his hobby but also his passion. In 1991, he joined an IT company, KAMI, founded by his ex-professor. At KAMI, Kaspersky was responsible for antivirus programme development – a new division with a lot of potential

[3] Ibid., p. 5.

but no revenue. Soon he invited his old classmate Alexey De Mont De Rique, a promising product manager, and Vadim Bogdanov, a talented programmer, to join the company.

The first antivirus programme developed by the team was named AVP. However, it was not the first antivirus product on the Russian market. Aidstest had been created in 1988 and by 1991 had a 90 per cent market share. But AVP had a few as yet unheard of features, including a user interface and a split-off between base and software. In addition, the product was bilingual (English and Russian), as Kaspersky could already see its global potential. His assumption would turn out to be correct. In 1994, AVP was tested by the University of Hamburg and acknowledged as the best in the world.

In the same year Natalya Kaspersky, Eugene's then-wife, joined the team as a sales manager to develop sales channels and partner networks. It was Natalya who, in 1997, persuaded Eugene and his partners to leave KAMI and create their own company. And it was also Natalya who insisted on naming the company 'Kaspersky Lab'. Eugene confirmed to us that he was against using his own name as a brand but gave in because of the growing recognition he was receiving.

Soon the company's share of the Russian market was 10 per cent, but its founders were already seeking opportunities abroad. Kaspersky Lab launched its global operations by selling white-label technology to other vendors. This model allowed it to sell internationally without significant investment in marketing and promotion. It was a natural strategy for the young company, which managed to establish a foothold and a reputation in the IT security industry thanks to its success in the University of Hamburg test, participation in industry exhibitions (such as CeBIT) and its publications in *Virus Bulletin*.

In 1999, Kaspersky Lab opened its first sales office abroad. It chose Cambridge in the United Kingdom, but this initial overseas venture was unsuccessful for a number of reasons: the conservative UK market, a series of hiring mistakes and a lack of necessary experience. During this period the company also made its first attempt to launch in the United States. The first manager, a local recruit, turned out to be a fraud, and the second, sent from Russia, a failure. However, Kaspersky and his team did not give up their dream of conquering the increasingly appealing US market and continued to broaden and strengthen their network of overseas partners.

The next year, the company held its first partner conference in its Moscow HQ, attended by 15 international collaborators. As a result, Kaspersky Lab negotiated exclusive distribution in its partners' territories in return for increased discounts. This model turned out to be extremely beneficial for both parties.

In 2003, Kaspersky Lab opened an office in Germany. This would be the first confident step in an explosive two-year international expansion, during which offices would be opened in France, Italy, Spain and Japan. Kaspersky Lab now had 250 employees, most of them based in the Moscow HQ. Russia generated 40 per cent of revenues, while other countries accounted for the remaining 60 per cent – and counting.

It was in 2005 that Kaspersky Lab decided to attack the highly competitive consumer computer-security market in the United States and hired a local manager, Stephen Orenberg. It seemed crazy to compete against such industry giants as Symantec, McAfee and Trend Micro. Most retailers saw antivirus software as a commodity and already had three or four vendors in this category. *Bloomberg Businessweek* published an article entitled 'Does the US Need Another Antivirus Company?' But they answered their own question positively, admitting that the Russian newcomer had something to offer. First, speed. Kaspersky Lab was the first company in the world to put out daily updates – as often as once an hour in 2004 (equivalent to more than 600 per month). In comparison, Symantec, Trend Micro and McAfee had an average of 30 updates per month or even fewer. Second, the right target group. Kaspersky Lab focused on the end consumers and small and medium enterprises (SMEs), a segment almost ignored by the large competitors, who made most of their money from huge corporate clients. And last but not least, pricing strategy. Orenberg made the decision to ignore price and marketing wars and simply charge the highest price. He thought that this market was looking for a premium product – and hit the mark. As a result Kaspersky Lab's market share in the United States rose to 4.6 per cent in 2008. Two years later, Kaspersky Lab was number one in retail sales in the United States, having overtaken its notable competitors.

In spite of these remarkable results the organization was facing internal problems. The new version of Kaspersky Anti-Virus 4.0 launched in 2004 was not up to scratch. It was slow and had an unacceptable number of bugs. The whole programme architecture had to be redesigned, and the launch of version 5.0 was cancelled. The company had failed to meet the very quality standards that gave it an edge. The reasons were rooted in the company's rapid growth. When the number of employees increased dramatically, the company tried to implement new management structures with well-designed business processes. The one-time 'community of free programmers' grew into a corporate bureaucracy. Kaspersky Lab pulled itself out of the technological crisis by completely restructuring its R&D function and redesigning its product architecture. In 2006, Kaspersky Anti-Virus 6.0 was successfully launched.

The next big challenge took the form of a managerial crisis. Natalya Kaspersky, who had divorced Eugene in 2001, stepped down as CEO of Kaspersky Lab. However, she remained the second-largest shareholder and wanted to continue participating in the company's governance. In 2007, to mitigate the escalating tension, a board of directors was established – with Natalya as chair. Eugene took over as CEO, while Evgeny Buyakin, the former CFO, was promoted to COO.

Now Kaspersky decided to shift to a robust holding structure with offices around the world. Local partner offices were to be bought out or closed. The previous business model, with its focus on a strong partnership network had been very successful when the company was smaller. But with the revenue growth, local offices had begun to compete with each other. In 2007, all offices were grouped into five regions (Western Europe, EEMEA, the Americas, Asia-Pacific (APAC) and Japan) – with reporting lines to headquarters in Moscow.

After Natalya's resignation she took the lead in daughter company InfoWatch and sought to cash out her shares in Kaspersky Lab. Natalya persuaded Eugene to take the company public. They started to prepare for an IPO, but the world economic crisis of 2008 put it on hold. Natalya still wanted to sell her shares, and in 2011 General Atlantic, a US-based private equity firm, paid US$200 million to buy 20 per cent of the company (most of these shares were owned by Natalya). However, a year later Eugene bought back the stake and retired the shares. The reasons behind the move were well articulated by Kaspersky: he did not want to lose control over his company. In his own words, public companies (and the ultimate goal of General Atlantic was an IPO) are 'too slow in decision making'.[4] Moreover he believed that going public would kill the unique culture of the company. General Atlantic understood that with such a stubborn shareholder it might be impossible to achieve their goals. Today, Eugene Kaspersky is still the controlling shareholder of the company.

In 2016, Kaspersky Lab was present in almost 200 countries and territories, had 32 regional offices, employed about 3,600 people and provided protection for over 400 million individual and 270,000 corporate clients worldwide. Its global revenue was about US$620 million (Kaspersky Lab does not publish audited financial results).

Innovations and Threats

Ever since 1994, when Kaspersky AVP was acknowledged as the best security software by the University of Hamburg, the company has maintained its technological leadership. As Kaspersky Lab reported in 2016, its products participated in 78 independent reviews and took first place 55 times, while 70 tests ranked Kaspersky Lab in the top three. The company was also named as the 'leader' by three major international analytical agencies (IDC, Gartner and Forrester).

In 2016, Kaspersky Lab had more than 1,000 R&D specialists (one-third of the company's employees), whereas in 2005 it had only 50. In those days, the antivirus research team used manual techniques. Today it is one of the most efficient antimalware research units in the industry (some experts say that competitors' R&D teams have three times more staff).

The Global Research and Analysis Team (GReAT) – a unique, worldwide group of top-notch cybersecurity experts – was created in 2008. The main goal of this elite group is to investigate new cyberattacks and find ways to fight them. In 2016, GReAT consisted

[4] M. Palmer, 'A Tech Tycoon Who Values Privacy', *The Financial Times*, 25 September 2012.

of 40-plus experts working in Europe, Russia, the Americas, Asia and the Middle East. GReAT is considered one of the company's best assets. So is the Kaspersky Security Network (KSN), launched in 2009. This is a complex distributed infrastructure dedicated to processing cybersecurity-related data streams from about 60 million voluntary participants across the globe. KSN is based on cloud technologies and ensures faster and more effective protection against the latest cybersecurity threats.

Kaspersky Lab's never-ending innovation is a reaction to the increasing complexity and density of cyberattacks. During the last ten years, a whole new industry of cybercrimes has emerged. Malware, spam, distributed denial-of-service (DDoS) attacks, cyberespionage and other online threats have made billions of dollars for their perpetrators. Moreover, the phenomenon has escalated into a problem of national security. In 2010, the 'Stuxnet' worm attacked Iran's nuclear system and became one of the most famous cyberweapons targeted at the fundamental infrastructure of a country. Stuxnet was recognized as a nation-state cyberespionage campaign, which has prompted the world's leading powers to add cyberweapons to their armoury.

In 2012, a Kaspersky Lab team was the first to discover 'Flame', which they described as one of the most complex threats ever uncovered. In this case the target was not state facilities but private data in Middle Eastern countries. Kaspersky Lab also found that Stuxnet and Flame have the same origin. At a conference in Tel Aviv around this time, Kaspersky said to the audience.

> I'm afraid that in the future there will be other countries in this game. It's only software. Maybe hacktivists will become cyber terrorists. And maybe the traditional terrorists will be in touch with the cyber terrorists.[5]

Since then the threat has evolved further. In 2016, Kaspersky Lab experts discovered that every fourth targeted attack they detected was aimed at industrial victims. And two in five computers related to the technological infrastructure of industrial enterprises faced cyberattacks.

[5] K. Vick, 'Finder of Flame Virus Tells Israel to Stop Before It's Too Late', *Time*, 6 June 2012.

International Expansion

How on earth did Kaspersky Lab, a small Russian company, realize its founders' global dreams? One of its secrets of success is always to view a disadvantage as a possibility. Kaspersky Lab executives believe that being an international company with Russian origins is a huge advantage. The reason is simple: the former leaders in the cybersecurity industry are big American companies that have always had a strong focus on the US market. The best other countries could hope for in their heyday was minor adaptation and high-level localization. In contrast, Kaspersky Lab did not have the option of relying on its underdeveloped domestic market and began looking overseas early in its development.

But how did the company succeed in these international markets? The best clue to its global success was provided by Orenberg, former president of Kaspersky Lab Americas, when he was first interviewed by Kaspersky: '*Localability*'. This means that the company has relied heavily on local knowledge in identifying ways of marketing and adapting to the local culture in each of its new territories. Meanwhile, most companies adhere to a 'not invented here' philosophy and adopt a 'one size fits all' model dictated by their domestic markets.

In 2007, Kaspersky Lab's brand was almost unknown outside of Russia, in spite of solid cash flows from across the globe. But after the switch from selling licenses to selling products, the need to create an international brand became acute. The cheapest and most effective solution by far was public relations (PR). In 2006, there were only three people in the PR department of Kaspersky Lab. Today there are almost 60 professionals around the world. The strategy was to catch the interest of the specialist media with top-notch innovative products and then expand to the mass audience. The company's Security Analyst Summit, organized for the first time in 2007, has become a global event, attracting hundreds of participants every year. For the mass audience the message changed slightly. Rather than emphasizing the advantages of its product, the company highlighted the problems of the consumer as well as its role as 'the good guy who came to save and protect you'.

Were the company's Russian roots an obstacle on the road to international expansion? Kaspersky says not. From day one the company decided to promote not just itself but also Russian R&D engineers in general. Certainly in some countries, the Russian background of the company was more favourable than in others. For example, in Germany the professionalism of Russian scientists and engineers is widely recognized. As a result Kaspersky Lab has 74 per cent brand recognition there for its consumer products. In the United States the company was less active in promoting its Russian origins but equally never made any attempts to hide them. For computer geeks, a Russian antivirus vendor was cool and exotic, while also being credible enough for an average consumer in an office in Boston or Seattle. The same was true in the United Kingdom. Asia, however, was more open to a Russian company. Asian consumers also pay more attention to recommendations from local companies, so developing a strong local network was a crucial step towards conquering the Asian market. In Latin America, in contrast, the best results were achieved through PR campaigns with endorsements from big international companies. Latin Americans also seemed to feel a connection with the Russian roots of Kaspersky Lab.

However, sometimes Kaspersky Lab still faces issues with its Russian background. In 2008, *The Guardian* apologized for mistakenly naming Eugene a 'KGB man',[6] but this was just the beginning. After much gossip and an article in *Wired*[7] claiming that Eugene had connections with the Russian security services, he published a comprehensive denial.[8] He confirmed that his company shares its unique technological expertise and experience with law enforcement agencies and assists in investigations. But it does so not only with the Federal Security Service (FSB) but also with Interpol, Europol and others.

---

[6] J. Schofield, 'The Russian Defense against Global Cybercrime', *The Guardian*, 31 January 2008.

[7] N. Shachtman, 'Russia's Top Cyber Sleuth Foils US Spies, Helps Kremlin Pals', *Wired*, 23 July 2012.

[8] E. Kaspersky, 'What *Wired* Is Not Telling You', *Nota Bene: Eugene Kaspersky's Official Blog*, 25 July 2012.

In 2015, *Bloomberg Businessweek* published an article with the scary title 'The Company Securing Your Internet Has Close Ties to Russian Spies', in which it claimed again that Kaspersky had worked for the KGB and that Kaspersky Lab was 'the most prominent cyber security business with close ties to the Russian government'[9] to also have 'access' to consumers' data. In a characteristically emotional manner, Eugene Kaspersky published a response,[10] accusing *Bloomberg* of bad journalism. Nevertheless, these publications and subsequent rumours of Russia hacking the US elections had a negative impact on the company's image and sales.

The ongoing economic boom in Asia has made the APAC region a market that is both fast growing and challenging. Kaspersky Lab is prepared for this, offering a comprehensive line of full security solutions backed up by a strong regional team. Nowadays Kaspersky Lab's total brand awareness in APAC countries is more than 60 per cent.

For every geographically dispersed company the issue of local management is extremely important. Kaspersky Lab promptly recognized that the key to success is strong local management with deep knowledge of the national market. The company invested heavily in hiring the right people and broadening its partner network.

However, for a very long period of time it had no foreign executives in Moscow. The situation changed when the growth rate went double-digit. To compete with the industry leaders Kaspersky Lab needed to strengthen its executive team but had no time to grow future leaders from within. As a result Moscow HQ hired a number of world-class international managers at the C-suite level (CMO, CFO etc.), who brought valuable expertise to the company. Although Kaspersky Lab had a successful track record in hiring and retaining talent for its offices abroad, at HQ it simply did not work. Cultures clashed immediately. Eugene soon concluded, 'We had the illusion that we could invite western

[9] C. Matlack, M. Riley and J. Robertson, 'The Company Securing Your Internet Has Close Ties to Russian Spies', *Bloomberg Businessweek*, 19 March 2015

[10] E. Kaspersky, 'A Practical Guide to Making Up a Sensation', *Nota Bene: Eugene Kaspersky's Official Blog*, 20 March 2015

managers to Russia. This was a total meltdown. We made two futile attempts. Now we are trying to find stars within the company. If we don't have enough, we will hire outsiders. But if these outsiders are located abroad we'll leave them there.'[11] Today there are no foreign managers in the Moscow executive team. Some Russians work in regional offices, but most employees, including managers, are local.

Organizational Structure

Since 2007 Kaspersky Lab seems to have been engaged in a process of endless change as far as organizational structure is concerned. This is hardly surprising. Between 2004 and 2011 its revenues increased fourfold. The structure that suited the needs of a US$200 million business became dysfunctional for a US$667 million company.

Initially the organizational structure was flat, with every local office reporting directly to headquarters in Moscow. But when the number of international offices reached 20, the need to create a new level in the hierarchy became evident. All markets were shared between five regional hubs. However this structure soon proved unstable. Some offices began to compete against others in the same region and had to be transferred to another. Sometimes the reasons for transfer were attributed to cross-cultural differences – some countries simply did not want to report to particular regional headquarters. As the turbulence continued – both inside and outside the company – the management board experimented further with the structure of the company. But the overall trend was always towards increased centralization.

All of the other major players in the cybersecurity market have grown by buying innovative companies. For example, since 2000 Symantec has made 48 acquisitions at an average price of US$552 million. Kaspersky is strictly against this way of doing business. 'It [acquisition] ruins the company's morale. Engineers want to innovate, but when you acquire companies it says to them they are not good enough to innovate themselves,'[12] he told

---

[11] Dorofeev and Kostylyova, *Kaspersky's Principle*, p. 43.
[12] Palmer, 'A Tech Tycoon Who Values Privacy'.

the *Financial Times*. The biggest acquisition in Kaspersky Lab's history is an office building in Moscow, partially leased to other companies.

For almost a decade Kaspersky Lab did not have to face the issue of corporate governance, as its shareholders managed the company directly and, in most cases, harmoniously. But in 2007, when Eugene replaced Natalya as CEO of the company, she remained the second-largest shareholder – and the balance was lost. The board of directors was created primarily to allow Natalya to participate in making key business decisions and to use her invaluable experience, gained over 10 years in the company's senior management team. As already mentioned, Natalya became the chair. The board also included Eugene, as CEO; Alexey De Mont De Rique; and six executive directors (CFO, business development director, and the heads of regional headquarters respectively). After the deal with General Atlantic, when Natalya sold her stake, she left the board and Eugene took over as chair. General Atlantic received one seat on the board, but the overall number of directors was reduced to five.

Corporate Culture

Kaspersky Lab has a strong 'geek' culture, typical of a young tech company. Corporate folklore says that geeks all over the world have the same unorthodox values system. They do not care greatly about money (provided their salaries are in line with the market, i.e. fair) but are energized by complex tasks and challenging goals. Besides this, for them it is important to work for a company with a hip and widely recognized brand name rather than a 'corporate monster'. The main thing is to feel part of the global tech community, to be state of the art. In Kaspersky Lab such people not only have an opportunity to work in a technology-driven company but can also participate in international cybersecurity events as representatives of the global industry's 'thought leader'.

The average age within the company is just 34. One reason is that programming is like professional sport in that the main breakthroughs are achieved by programmers between 25 and 35 years of age. For example, the former CTO was appointed to his position when he was just over 30. This youthfulness makes acquisition, retention and development of rising stars crucial for the company. Contrary to popular myth, Kaspersky Lab has never employed ex-hackers or virus-writing programmers. As its executives point out, the best analogy is with the police, who never hire ex-criminals. These are simply different kinds of people.

Kaspersky Lab seeks to shape a fun culture for its employees all over the world. Eugene says that the best example to emulate is Google, a bright, dynamic company that brings together the very best minds. On the opposite side is IBM, a boring corporate giant. A fun culture manifests itself in many ways: casual dress code, open-plan offices, parties, events for children and so forth. But frequent and open communication is always at the heart. As one former team member says, 'There is a big illusion that R&D specialists and programmers are solo players. In any technology, company teamwork is essential. Horizontal relationships matters more than vertical.'[13]

According to *Forbes* magazine's ranking of 'The Best Enterprise Software Companies and CEOs to Work for in 2014'[14] (based on PricewaterhouseCoopers' survey of the 'Global 100 Software Leaders' and Glassdoor data), Kaspersky Lab was the sixteenth most attractive international software company (with Microsoft just behind). Some 79 per cent of employees are ready to recommend Kaspersky Lab to their friends, while 85 per cent say that their CEO is the best role model for the whole company.

Kaspersky's Leadership

Although many external observers are puzzled by Kaspersky's business success – and some even attribute it to 'shadow shareholders', 'support from the secret services' and other factors beyond Eugene's control – the entrepreneur knows his own secret: 'First, I sometimes guess future trends in the world of viruses, trends in computer-related risks, and we manage to react faster than others. Second, our capacity to develop software that catches viruses better and faster than others. Third, my ability to put

---

[13] In interview with authors.
[14] L. Columbus, 'The Best Enterprise Software Companies and CEOs to Work for in 2014', *Forbes.com*, 18 March 2014.

together a team. And, of course, pure luck.'[15] Kaspersky considers personal humility a fundamental trait of a successful business leader: 'Megalomania is the biggest risk [...] It can be cured only at the early stages, and – if it is not – it's really bad for both the leader and the company. A good friend of mine caught me at the second stage (of megalomania) and cured me. Since then I have developed immunity to it.'[16]

Humble, inspired by a good cause, visionary, technically savvy, people-oriented and approachable – that is how Eugene Kaspersky sees his own leadership. Now let's listen to some of his followers:

Eugene has great intuition. From his initial interest in antivirus software to specific product offerings he made right strategic moves.

Kaspersky makes people work hard and feel good about it. He walks around and says 'Back to work, everyone'. Employees repeat this slogan and follow.

Kaspersky pays a lot of attention to hiring and firing. We have an elaborate hiring process, but at the end of it he spends hours interviewing candidates, discussing all possible and impossible issues and assessing their fit with the company's culture. Eugene does not hesitate to fire people when he feels they underperform or do not live our values. It creates productive tension in the office.

Eugene does not manage people in a traditional sense – most likely he does not know how to do it. He pays a lot of attention to selection and then leaves employees alone, but makes himself available to people who proactively seek his help.

Kaspersky's major role is to set direction and establish standards for other employees. He aims very high and he expects every employee to have ambition; he works hard and he expects everyone to work hard; he learns and he expects everyone to learn; he does not care about the form but the substance, and he expects others to do the same. He instils his norms by walking around, talking to people and working with them.

Kaspersky has a lot of courage. Since the very beginning he has taken on problems he does not know how to solve and learns what is required to solve them. Kaspersky Lab works in the same way.

Eugene Kaspersky may come across as a spacey computer geek and laissez-faire manager, but he knows and controls all major processes in the organization. He is deeply involved and keeps his finger on the company's pulse.

[15] Dorofeev and Kostylyova, *Kaspersky's Principle*, p. 125.
[16] Ibid., p. 128.

Kaspersky is very Russian in many ways, but he has a global mindset when it comes to business. He sees the whole world as his playground and he wants to leave his mark on it. And he sets global performance standards for the employees. If you want to work for Kaspersky Lab in any meaningful position you need to be world class.[17]

Eugene Kaspersky has a rather unusual biography for a Russian entrepreneur of the 1990s and 2000s. The only child of a middle-class family, he excelled in mathematics from his earliest years in school, was selected to study at the elite high school of Moscow State University, graduated from an elite university training programme for the Soviet secret services, worked at the research institute of the Ministry of Defence and wrote his first antivirus programme at the age of 23. Since then Kaspersky has dedicated himself to what he and his company do best – protecting the cyberworld from various threats.

Talking of people and events that shaped his mindset and leadership style, Kaspersky mentions Singaporean leader Lee Kwan Yew, Soviet mathematician Andrey Kolmogorov, global entrepreneur Richard Branson and Kaspersky's own mother, who 'moulded and educated me and gave me the right direction' and who 'still helps me with problems I cannot solve at work'.[18]

Kaspersky Lab employees all agree that their boss's social intelligence, technical skills and ambition are the three principal traits that make him an outstanding business leader. But Kaspersky himself – ever humble – considers tenacity his main asset: 'I am not so much talented but rather persistent. If I want to do something I will do it, no matter how much time and effort it will take. I will be hitting and hitting the same rock until it cracks.'[19]

[17] In interviews with authors.
[18] Dorofeev and Kostylyova, *Kaspersky's Principle*, p. 125.
[19] Ibid., p. 125.

6

Alexander Dyukov: Quiet Transformation of Gazprom Neft

*I play to win, whether during practice or a real game. And
I will not let anything get in the way of me and my competitive
enthusiasm to win.*

— Michael Jordan

*Progress comes to those who train and train; reliance on secret
techniques will get you nowhere.*

— Morihei Ueshiba, Aikido founder

Alexander Dyukov, the CEO of Gazprom Neft, is the least typical
of our athletic leaders. He is an introvert – meticulous, extremely
polite and quiet. 'When we first started working with Alexander,'
recalls Kirill Kravchenko, one of his deputies, 'it was hard to
decipher his reactions – whether he approved or disapproved of
a particular proposal. We tried to "read" his feedback, even got
together [to discuss it] in small groups, but still couldn't succeed.'
Yet Dyukov is as tough as can be, his ambition for winning is
unparalleled and his adaptability is enviable.

No other protagonist of this book typifies the '*Cool Head*'
dimension of athletic leadership as well as Dyukov. When oil prices
dropped and the Russian economy plunged into a sharp depression
in 2008, members of his team called for a swift revision of business
strategy and drastic measures to cut costs, pointing to other
companies that had already launched such measures. Dyukov stayed
cool. He explained that he did not see any fundamental reasons

for prolonged low oil prices and did not want to be led in his decision-making by temporary factors. Gazprom Neft cancelled some projects but remained committed to its growth strategy. Oil prices rebounded in less than 12 months. In 2016, in the second year of another Russian recession, when oil prices started to pick up, some of Dyukov's subordinates suggested that the time had come to curtail Gazprom Neft's drive to improve operational. The CEO answered with a firm *nyet* and explained, 'The 50-dollar prices are there to stay and the only way to win is to become more efficient.'[1]

Among his subordinates Alexander Dyukov is famous for *never being satisfied* with results, people, plans and actions. One of his deputies shares his view: 'From time to time I ask myself the same question. Why don't we pause for a while? Why not celebrate success and praise those who achieved it? But then I continue pursuing a new goal and I feel good. I think Dyukov understands that we need to be challenged on a continuous basis. Otherwise we will get bored and lose motivation.'[2] Dissatisfaction with the status quo is behind many of Dyukov's most important decisions – including the one he made in 2006 to become CEO of an oil company, which launched his most ambitious leadership project to date.

In October 2006, Dyukov, CEO of the petrochemical company Sibur, accepted an offer to head Gazprom Neft, a company that owned several large oilfields in Western Siberia and two refineries, and that had recently been acquired by Gazprom. When he shared the news with some of his close colleagues, they thought he was crazy. Why leave a company that in the three years of his leadership had emerged from bankruptcy and had tripled its revenues for an organization with declining revenues and production volumes? Why venture into a new industry well known for suspicion towards outsiders and populated by independently minded oil 'barons' running their production subsidiaries in a semiautonomous way?

In early 2017, Gazprom Neft announced record profits for the previous year, making it the most efficient oil company in Russia. By that time Dyukov was not simply its CEO but was also president

---

[1] In interview with authors.
[2] In interview with authors.

of Zenit Football Club and one of the most respected business leaders in the country. Asked about the secret of Gazprom Neft's success, he responded, 'There is one factor – work. Our key advantage is that we are proactive, not indifferent. We are focused on development. We have assembled a team such that anyone who has these qualities has a chance to prove himself.'[3] As for the CEO's role, he summed it up in three key tasks: 'Determining strategy, [handling] government relations and external communications, and supporting the group [management].'[4]

Born in St Petersburg, Dyukov as a child was interested in football and fencing but at some point opted for the latter. He went to a school that specialized in training future champions, although football always remained a part of his life. At Sibur, Dyukov made football obligatory for all top managers, regularly arranging soccer games and actively participating in them. He brought this tradition with him to Gazprom Neft, where football and sport are taken quite seriously. In 2008, Dyukov became the president of Zenit St Petersburg, in which Gazprom owns a controlling stake, and since then has never missed a single game. In addition to football, he boxes, runs and goes to the gym.

He grew up in the Leningrad of the 1970s and 1980s, typified by communal apartments with several families sharing a kitchen and a bathroom, street thugs, defence manufacturing, the seaport and some of the best museums in the world. While acknowledging the city's influence on him, in his typical manner, he declines to expand.

Though Dyukov graduated from the Shipbuilding University with a degree in auto-engineering, he almost never worked as an engineer. During the perestroika years, Leningrad (which reverted to its former name, St Petersburg, in 1991) became a hotbed for joint ventures (JV). After graduating, Dyukov worked in one of these JVs, creating software products, then in the lumber trade, before joining the Seaport. In the turbulent 1990s he had to conduct difficult negotiations with trade unions, pay back bad debts and work with a new wave of businessmen who hailed from

[3] In interview with authors.
[4] In interview with authors.

all walks of life, ranging from members of the security forces to criminals.

His competitive personality found a natural home in business. In big business, as in big-time sport, there is always an opponent, rules to follow and objective indicators to measure results. The continuous benchmarking performed by Gazprom Neft is in many ways a means of finding the worthiest opponents and creating a system by which to determine a winner.

Another trademark is the high expectations he imposes on himself and his subordinates, many of whom say that the CEO is stingy with praise but makes up for it by extending a high degree of autonomy. 'Dyukov is a restless person who demands a lot from himself and others. He rarely praises his subordinates, but never praises himself either. He delegates a lot, and you try to live up to that trust,'[5] explains Vadim Yakovlev, one of his management team.

Dyukov is constantly raising the bar for his company, even if the board of directors or the market situation does not demand it, and leads his team to meet these goals. 'For Alexander Dyukov, the most important value is development – that is his personal value,'[6] says Yakovlev. Development does not stop at the company level. Dyukov explains,

> The company has changed – it is a different company now in terms of volumes, scope, technologies, influence on the industry. We try to develop not just our company but the industry as well through legislation and initiatives for import substitution, helping the innovative community. This is its own kind of public service, our contribution to the country's development.[7]

Building a Foundation

It was a combination of his previous performance at Sibur and the trust of Gazprom CEO Alexey Miller (they had worked together

---

[5] In interview with authors.
[6] In interview with authors.
[7] In interview with authors.

at the St Petersburg Seaport from 1996 to 1999) that gave Dyukov carte blanche to bring change to Gazprom Neft.

Unlike his predecessor (who had exhorted executives to 'work as you've been working. I'm not advocating that such a sound team should undergo serious changes.'[8]), Dyukov began by changing the management team. He appointed Sibur executives Vadim Yakovlev, Abdulla Karaev and Alexander Krylov to the key positions of CFO, director of procurement and head of regional sales. Other members of the team came from the market, including Kravchenko, who left Yukos to head the HR and Organizational Development unit. 'It was more like assembling by hand, bit by bit. In the end we got a very diverse team,'[9] says Baranov. But there was one quality common to all of them: a results-oriented, proactive approach to business.

Not all of the remaining Sibneft executives shared these values. Some quit and others were asked to leave. The only member of the 10-member management board to stay at Gazprom Neft was Anatoly Cherner, vice president (downstream) responsible for Refining, Logistics and Sales. 'Cherner is an example of how a mature leader can change. He changed his mindset and style and is now one of the symbols of the new Gazprom Neft,'[10] says Kravchenko. In 2017, the Gazprom Neft management board consisted of eleven members – three (including Dyukov) worked at Sibur, three had worked (at different times) at Gazprom, one was from the Sibneft era and the rest came from other companies or government agencies.

While assembling his executive team, Dyukov started to make changes at the second and third levels of management. Sibneft's regional operations had been given a high level of autonomy, and managers did not really consider themselves part of the overall company. Gazprom Neft acquired a recruiting agency to help find talent and incorporated it into the HR department. 'We called upon those we had known before, for example Yukos veterans, and combed the market to find the best. Of course, not everyone

[8] N. Grib and N. Skornyakova, 'Anti-crisis Executive Is Sent to Sibneft', *Kommersant*, 19 October 2005.
[9] In interview with authors.
[10] In interview with authors.

rose to the challenge, but I believe it made a huge difference,'[11] recalls Kravchenko.

Dyukov changed the company's architecture. Profit centres were established and later organized into divisions (he had implemented a similar system at Sibur). 'Dyukov's management style complemented this approach. Having defined the business structure, he handed over the management of these divisions to their heads, delegating to them the supervision of and responsibility for the financial results, says Yakovlev, first deputy CEO. The CEO's attention at this stage was primarily on creating a team and culture and formulating key business indicators. By 2015 he could say, 'Now everything has been established and functions independently [of me].'[12]

As part of his 'unification' of Gazprom Neft, company-wide policies and procedures were developed. This started with the offices – a single rented building for all employees at headquarters – and later extended to basic policies for project management, strategic planning, informational security, risk management and subsidiaries. Dyukov declared war on bureaucracy and initiated the transition to electronic documentation. In particular, he launched SAP HR and significant changes to the procurement system and financial control.

In 2007, Gazprom Neft introduced a performance management system, UPC (pronounced 'oo-pe-tse', a Russian version of management by objectives (MBO)), which had come to Russia through a global service provider, Schlumberger and oil major BP. Strategic goals were cascaded down to units, departments, divisions and subsidiaries, and ultimately transformed into tasks for individual managers at different levels. Implementation required rebuilding the organizational structure of the company: grades were developed and a key performance indicator (KPI) system and annual performance reviews were introduced. One year later, a long-term incentive scheme for the top management was developed. 'Without this tool, I simply couldn't manage my people,'[13] said Dyukov.

---

[11] In interview with authors.
[12] In interview with authors.
[13] E. Mazneva, 'More Generous Than Abramovich', *Vedomosti*, 30 October 2007.

The drive for efficiency, as well as high oil prices, led to a significant improvement in performance. By 2009, EBITDA reached US$7.9 billion and net income US$4.6 billion. Yakovlev, then CFO, attributed two-thirds of that growth to management's efforts.

However, the global financial crisis of 2009 and the fall in oil prices hit the oil industry and Gazprom Neft hard. In 2009, EBITDA and net income fell by more than 30 per cent and revenues dropped by 28 per cent. Dyukov remained calm – the company quickly optimized its investment programme – and CAPEX was reduced from US$3.5 to US$2.5 billion and costs reduced by over US$260 million in one year. Operating results continued to improve: oil and gas extraction rose by 3.1 per cent, volumes refined increased by 17.6 per cent, and average daily output began to grow, which, given the slump in the industry, was an unprecedented achievement.

Growth

From the outset, Dyukov made growth – in terms of the operational and financial indicators and volume of crude production – his top priority. In 2010, Gazprom Neft, with the help of McKinsey, developed a new strategy for 2020, dubbed '100-70-40', that is, 100 million tons of hydrocarbons, 70 million tons of refining and 40 million tons in sales to end consumers each year. Revenue and net income were expected to double by 2020.

He articulated two other ambitions: to provide the highest total return for shareholders and to be one of Russia's top three most efficient vertically integrated oil producers. In 2013, the strategy was updated, some targets increased and the horizon extended to 2025. 'Initially, the strategy was put into place by an authoritative CEO decision – it reflected a level of his ambition and more intuitive understanding of the scale of the business desired,'[14] Yakovlev recalls. 'It was hard to say whether the strategy was shared by all; it was more that "the management decided",'[15] notes Ekaterina Matskevich, HR director in 2011–14.

[14] In interview with authors.
[15] In interview with authors.

For many in the company the new strategy was an enigma. Dyukov challenged top management to get buy-in from the whole organization. Gazprom Neft conducted a number of strategy sessions at which executives and mid-level managers discussed how to reach seemingly unattainable targets. Yakovlev recalls,

> During the sessions on operationalizing strategic targets and Gazprom Neft trends, we came to understand that the strategy was realistic. To achieve 100 million tons of production, we would need to grow at 7 per cent a year. This was, of course, higher than the industry average, but lower than what we had already done.[16]

Later, senior managers established a clear link between strategic goals and medium-term planning. At annual meetings they discussed the contribution of the current year towards the strategic goals as well as shortcomings and measures to address them.

Organic Growth

The first priorities were to increase brownfield production through new technologies for hard-to-recover reserves and to develop new fields, including those in offshore and Arctic locations. In 2013, Goldman Sachs analysts estimated that Gazprom Neft had the best greenfield project portfolio on the Russian market and should be able to increase production by 35 per cent between 2013 and 2018.

Between 2010 and 2016, hydrocarbon production increased by 7 per cent every year. In 2016, it reached 86 million tons (see Table 6.1). Reserve life was 33 years. According to Dyukov, brownfield production would continue to be profitable even with a significant drop in the oil price, as production costs at brownfield sites were US$12–15 billion.

The company actively invested in modernizing its refineries. In 2013, Gazprom Neft transitioned to producing oil products to meet the highest emissions standards – Euro-5 – two years before this was legally required. The second modernization, in 2014, was aimed at increasing processing depth. In 2016, 42 million tons of

---

[16] In interview with authors.

oil were refined, putting Gazprom Neft in the top three largest oil companies in Russia.

For the third block of goals – sales to end consumers – Gazprom Neft divided its product portfolio into four segments (aviation fuel, bunker fuel, lubricants and other). In 2015, it became the market leader in both aviation and bunker fuel. Sales volumes in the premium segments rose from 14.2 million tons to 25 million tons by 2016. Simultaneously it worked intensely on its network of gas stations – rebranding and introducing loyalty programmes for customers, a corporate payment system for legal entities and a unified standard for customer service. As a result, between 2010 and 2014 Gazprom Neft doubled average daily sales volume per station (from 10.3 tons to 20 tons), becoming a market leader in this category.

Non-organic Growth

Gazprom Neft made its first acquisition at the end of 2007, purchasing a 50 per cent share in Tomskneft for US$3.6 billion (the other half belonged to Rosneft). This helped increase its proven reserves by 10 per cent. In 2009, parent company Gazprom gave the Novoportovskoye, Tazovskoye and Orenburgskoye oilfields to Gazprom Neft as part of an asset transfer.

Soon after Dyukov joined, Gazprom Neft began actively seeking to add refining capacity. In 2009, it acquired a controlling stake in Sibir Energy, which owned 50 per cent of the Moscow Oil Refinery and a share of a joint venture with Shell, with licenses for the development of eight oilfields and a network of service stations. The purchase of Sibir Energy was a remarkable deal for which it competed head-to-head with TNK-BP, which had been the first to make an offer. 'In order to stay in the running we had just a few hours to develop a counteroffer,' recalls Yakovlev. 'The deal was structurally complex. First we purchased a large chunk of stock on the market, then bought out major shareholders and then delisted the company. But by the end we understood that we could compete with the market leaders and complete major deals – and that was another way to grow the business.'[17]

---

[17] In interview with authors.

In February 2009, Gazprom Neft acquired a 51 per cent stake in the Serbian company Naftna Industrija Srbije, Petroleum Industry of Serbia (NIS), which produced 1 million tons of oil per year, with annual refining capacity of 7.3 million tons. Through the acquisition of NIS, Gazprom Neft intended to penetrate not just the Serbian market but also other European countries. In April 2009, through marketing and production synergies, the company acquired a refinery in Bari (Italy) from Chevron Global Energy.

At the end of 2009, Gazprom Neft became a member of the consortium to develop the Badra oilfield in Iraq, which had reserves of over two billion barrels. The following year, Gazprom Neft became the leader of the Russian consortium in the Junin-6 project in Venezuela and joined projects in Cuba and Equatorial Guinea.

Indeed, not all of Gazprom Neft's acquisition attempts were successful. In 2008, the company was actively negotiating the acquisition of Russneft's oil assets (controlled by businessman Oleg Deripaska and state-owned Sberbank), but the deal fell through. 'At the time, it was upsetting, and it seemed like we didn't do all of our homework,' Dyukov reflects, 'but looking back, maybe it's good that we didn't buy them.'[18]

He remained convinced, however, that the future of all oil companies lay in partnerships:

> Joint ventures are a general trend in the world. We feel comfortable with different partners and don't enter partnerships with the desire to gain at the expense of the other side; we believe in 'win-win'.[19]

First Oil from the Arctic

In 2013, Gazprom asked Gazprom Neft to become an operator of the Prirazlomnoye oilfield project, and the company entered the icy waters of the Arctic – a move thought by many observers to be against the CEO's will.

[18] In interview with authors.
[19] In interview with authors.

The Arctic is believed to contain up to one-fifth of the world's total undiscovered hydrocarbon reserves, and Russia owns more than 40 per cent of the Arctic shell. Exploration started in the Soviet era, and in 1989, on the bed of the Pechora Sea, the Prirazlomnoye oilfield was discovered, with estimated reserves of 70 million tons, in an area where ice is present for two-thirds of the year, temperatures can fall below −50°C and the polar night lasts for two months.

Gazprom had started to develop technology and machinery to operate the field since 1995, initially in partnership with BHP Petroleum and Rosneft. Following disagreements, both partners exited the project. In 2012, Gazprom Neft was being asked to operate what was arguably the most difficult oilfield in the world − no other company had ever produced oil in such severe conditions. And the challenges did not stop with the climate.

In 2014, Gazprom Neft became sole owner of the project and assumed full responsibility. According to Gennady Lubin, general director of Gazprom Neft Shell, the Gazprom Neft subsidiary, they took all necessary steps to protect the environment, using unique technology to manage environmental risks. The company employed a zero-discharge system, which prevented drilling and production waste entering the sea (waste is pumped into special absorption wells or collected in tanks, and delivered to the shore for disposal). Land and marine ecosystems in the region were constantly monitored and fish populations replenished with help from fish farms. In 2014, Gazprom Neft joined the Arctic Oil Spill Response Technology Joint Industry Programme implemented by major oil and gas companies (BP, Chevron and ConocoPhillips) and conducted a large-scale training programme, Arctic 2014.

The first ever shipment of oil from offshore Arctic waters (branded ARCO) arrived in Europe in April 2014. Alexey Miller, CEO of Gazprom and chairman of Gazprom Neft, said that from that moment the investment in Prirazlomnoye began yielding returns. In 2017, Prirazlomnoye was producing 10,000 tons of oil daily, and at US$50 per barrel the project is returning money to shareholders.

Development of the Organization

In 2010, the Gazprom Neft management had a difficult choice: either obey the orders of its parent company Gazprom and move its headquarters to St Petersburg or challenge its majority shareholder and insist that it remain in Moscow. Several managers thought that the move would prompt the loss of a significant number of key employees and undermine the motivation of the rest. Dyukov had a different opinion: 'Stress – just like for an individual – is useful for a company. A change in scenery, the necessity of working in new conditions, helps develop skills and unite a team.'[20]

Moving the headquarters also made economic sense. The tax benefits offered by the St Petersburg authorities and lower office rental rates helped quickly recoup the significant cost. Ekaterina Matskevich, HR director during that time, recalls that once the decision was made, 'Dyukov made it clear the move should have a positive impact on the business. That was an extremely challenging goal. No other large company has ever moved its HQ away from Moscow.'[21] Dyukov made the move one of his priorities, and regularly checked on its progress, met with those who were having doubts and made quick decisions in uncertain situations. He even had the board of directors allocate extra funds to incentivize people and their families to relocate.

Gazprom Neft successfully dealt with the main risk: losing employees. The company did a lot to keep the team intact. It announced the upcoming move early on, determined who would not be moving to St Petersburg and paid them to help groom their successor. Two-thirds relocated, and Gazprom Neft did not want to move most of the remaining third. Matskevich says,

> The HQ relocation is a big change for the company and for its employees, for their lives and their mindsets. We felt that the move opened up our people, made them ready to embrace even more change, so we used this opportunity to launch other initiatives – transforming corporate culture, redesigning compensation and evaluation policies.[22]

Another key process at Gazprom Neft was benchmarking. Dyukov loves to compare – he is always interested in what others are doing and how to be better than they are, and benchmarking

---

[20] In interview with authors.
[21] In interview with authors.
[22] In interview with authors.

is one of the key processes at Gazprom Neft. 'We are constantly looking to overtake competitors – it's a culture of healthy competition,'[23] explains Kravchenko. Often, consultants helped with this. McKinsey, Bain and BCG worked with Gazprom Neft and presented best practices, but Gazprom Neft did a lot on its own. In 2011, the exploration and production unit decided to develop an index of operational efficiency for oil production, similar to the Solomon Associates index for refining. With help from Schlumberger, Gazprom Neft designed a set of metrics to analyse every cost element in oil production, adjusting for regional conditions and geological specifications.

Three major Russian oil companies – Lukoil, Rosneft and TNK-BP – supported Gazprom Neft and agreed to share their data to see how they matched up against the competition. 'We actively use this tool,' says Yakovlev. 'We evaluated which figures we should reach, have included them in our business plan and have created a road map for how we'll get there.'[24] However, over time, some companies stopped participating in the project. In 2015, Gazprom Neft was not able to pull together a pool of participants, so the company benchmarked internally between its own assets and joint ventures. According to Yakovlev, internal benchmarking helped identify discrepancies in results and highlight best practice.

Technology and Beyond

According to Dyukov, Gazprom Neft started by 'being more like integrators; using existing technologies as much as possible. Our approach was to take raw technologies and improve them ourselves.'[25] As the company developed, it created in-house technological capabilities, set up its own technology centre (NTC) staffed with the best oil engineers in the country and moved on to developing and deploying its own technology, primarily in exploration and production.

From 2012 Gazprom Neft has been actively building its digital capability. Dyukov says, 'I want digital technology to become a

---

[23] In interview with authors.
[24] In interview with authors.
[25] In interview with authors.

"productive force" at Gazprom Neft, not a supporting tool, which makes employees' work easier or more effective (that's easy), but a force that brings a different dynamic to the company, changes our business and production models.'[26]

Centres of expertise were a tool for technological development – every regional subsidiary was designated a centre of excellence in some important area. For example, Gazpromneft-Noyabrskneftegaz's expertise was technology to work with declining production, while Gazpromneft-Khantos's expertise was development of low-permeability reservoirs. Matskevich recalls,

> Every subsidiary won a 'gold medal' for accumulating and disseminating expert knowledge and best practices in an important area. There were no winners or losers. Each had its own specialization – we work more as a team than as competitors among assets.[27]

Experts and managers from different subsidiaries regularly participated in steering committees, where they shared their achievements, challenges and ideas. Experts from different subsidiaries often formed working groups to solve common problems and disseminate knowledge.

From 2013 to 2015, Gazprom Neft took its share of high-tech wells (horizontal wells, multistage fracking wells and multilateral horizontal wells) from 4 per cent to 35 per cent of the total amount drilled, making it one of Russia's industry leaders in this category. Its share of horizontal drilling in total volumes exceeded 46 per cent, a Russian record.

In 2013, with help from Accenture, it started work on the 'digital or smart field' project, a concept developed by Shell that allowed production to be managed through automation, using big data and integrating it into financial analysis. Extensive benchmarking was carried out among global companies. The project group visited the world's most innovative oilfields (in the Middle East) as well as the largest (in Indonesia). The task was not so much 'to steal and repeat at home' but to understand how innovation works in the world of oil production. 'Consultants helped us to understand

---

[26] In interview with authors.
[27] In interview with authors.

that it's not possible to take a template and implement it at home,' says Sergey Doktor. 'Each field is different. You need to develop your own recipe. Then you understand that it's all about people; the technology comes second.'[28]

Low oil prices and an economic downturn in Russia made technology even more important for achieving strategic goals. 'Before, we hoped acquisitions would ensure growth, but now it comes from new technologies and efficient management of available resources,'[29] notes Matskevich.

In addition to developing technology and company's employees to work with it, Gazprom Neft is actively involved in improving the quality of training for specialists in the industry and the entire economy. It founded a department at the St Petersburg Mining University. Its managers teach courses and exams at St Petersburg University (SPBU) and the city's University of Economics and Finance. Every year Gazprom Neft holds a case-study competition for oil production and refining, and in 2015, over 10,000 graduates and university students took part. The winners are invited to train at the company's R&D centre.

Gazprom Neft actively helps its new home city of St Petersburg as well as the 29 regions of the Russian Federation in which it has a presence. In 2010, a regional policy concept was accepted, involving a single collegial body – the Commission on Regional Policy – composed of representatives from different business units. In 2013, the 'Hometown' programme was launched, which was aimed at raising the quality of life in the cities where the company is present. In 2014, it had over 350 projects in five key areas: urban development, the creation and development of children's and recreational sports, education, development of the territory's cultural potential and, in the North, cooperation with indigenous populations.

Never Satisfied with Results

Between 2006 and 2016, Gazprom Neft's reserves more than doubled from 720 million tons to 1.6 billion tons, annual

---

[28] In interview with authors.
[29] In interview with authors.

hydrocarbons rose from 46 to 86 million tons in oil equivalent, and refining increased from 24 to 42 million tons. Gazprom Neft grew sales of oil products from 24 to 40 million tons, including 4.5 million tons of fuel through a network of 1,427 gas stations. The financial results followed operational performance, although the rouble's devaluation somewhat spoilt the picture.

Dyukov emphasizes the qualitative rather the quantitative side of Gazprom Neft's performance. According to him, the company has built a resource base similar to the ones of global oil majors: 'We don't yet have deep water oil fields, but all other types of reserves are present in our portfolio: heavy oil, oil sands, and natural gas.'[30] The company has an advanced technological capability, a professional and highly engaged workforce and a strong balance sheet. The CEO believes the 100 million ton production target will be achieved in one or two years and that all major elements of the current strategy will be implemented by then.

The new strategy has to deal with the challenges of a turbulent world and traditional industry facing a declining quality of its primary resources and increasing difficulty in reaching them, fierce competition from other sources of energy and hostility from many elements of society and the business community. Dyukov says that the strategy 'has to address technological change and digital disruption'.[31] The CEO thinks that the strategy itself will be flexible, open and ever-evolving rather than a traditional 10- or 15-year plan with set-in-stone numerical targets, multi-year strategic initiatives and investment projects.

Gazprom Neft is already implementing some elements of the future strategy, which has not been and perhaps may never become formalized in a corporate document. Its upstream block has 9 long-term technology-related programmes which include 86 active and over 60 potential projects. Programmes address such issues as exploration and drilling technologies, unconventional resources, oil rims' development and the development of fractured reservoirs. In exploration the company is developing a unique capability in deep basin modelling for prediction of major new deposits and optimization of field development. With

---

[30] In interview with authors.
[31] In interview with authors.

its help they aim to access up to 500 billion barrels of oil reserves in basin with complex tectonics, achieve 85 per cent success in exploration drilling and reduce costs in drilling development. According to Dyukov, 'accuracy in deposits modelling and consecutive accuracy of drilling should become our competitive advantage'.[32]

Both upstream and downstream blocks are developing digital technology using big data, predictive analytics and neurodynamics. The company introduced a mobile application for retail and wholesale customers which is being updated four to five times a month and has become very popular. On the basis of data analysis the sales division develops 'target value propositions' – specific offers for individual customers. For example, people who often buy beer, get discounts on the brew which are not available to other clients. Krylov explains, 'Big data and digital communication allow us to pass a middleman. Instead of spending money on advertising we reach customers directly with messages designed for them only. For example, we offered discounts to customers who had stopped buying from us. Seventy per cent of the population we have reached came back.'[33]

In 2016, Dyukov took a further step towards making Gazprom Neft a world-class organization: he announced plans to create a company-wide operations management system, OMS (Russian abbreviation SUOD). The project will take many years and will transform management practices, operational procedures and the corporate culture of Gazprom Neft, making it as efficient as the global industry leader: Exxon Mobil. According to the company, SUOD 'aims to organize the work of all enterprises and employees to make sure operations are safe, reliable and sustainable, and to secure the economic efficiency of the Company'.[34] For the CEO, the keywords are 'system' and 'operational efficiency'. He set up and chairs the OMS Committee, which consists of Gazprom Neft senior executives and invited experts; created a dedicated OMS implementation office; hired an industry veteran with BP experience, Evgeny Bulgakov, to run it; and appointed

---

[32] In interview with authors.
[33] In interview with authors.
[34] Gazprom Neft internal documents

dedicated compact OMS implementation offices in upstream and downstream.

As with many of Dyukov's initiatives the initial reaction at the company was mixed at best. 'Most companies turn to OMS when they face troubles – declining profitability, poor quality or low productivity. We are going from strength to strength, both operationally and financially. Why change?'[35] said a director of a service subsidiary. Others see the following in SUOD Dyukov's trademark approach: 'By giving us this huge challenge he does not let us to become complacent. It creates positive energy and unites people from different parts of the organization.'[36]

While Gazprom Neft's managers are trying to come to terms with SUOD, their CEO thinks about long-term future of the oil industry and appropriate positioning of its company. For years Dyukov advocated strict industry focus and declined all diversification proposals from within and from outside the company. Is the situation different today? Gazprom Neft has developed strong capabilities in complex large-scale project management, it knows how to operate joint ventures and it is rapidly acquiring digital acumen. With its financial prowess and strong talent pool shall the company explore opportunities outside of the industry, whose future looks more and more uncertain? Competition from alternative sources of energy; negative public opinion; and some governments' actions to restrict, if not outlaw, internal combustion engines, followed by automakers' extensive electric vehicles programmes create significant risks for the oil industry. Will it take the path of coal from a strategic resource to a commodity, or will it have its own trajectory? Gazprom Neft's CEO is thinking hard about these questions, but also studies Google's and Amazon's forays into unrelated markets and entertains an idea of limited-scale escapades outside of the oil industry.

[35] In interview with authors.
[36] In interview with authors.

Table 6.1 Gazprom Neft Performance (2006–16)

	2006	2007	2008	2009	2010	2011	2012	2013	2014	2015	2016
Financial indicators											
Revenue (RUB million)	548,585	582,405	842,008	766,546	995,286	1,029,803	1,232,649	1,267,603	1,408,238	1,467,943	1,545,608
Revenue (USD million)	20,176	22,768	33,870	24,166	32,772	33,654	38,045	38,227	35,118	23,081	23,006
EBITDA (RUB million)	154,330	159,517	198,010	162,280	197,587	271,289	305,124	316,463	300,761	345,160	402,277
EBITDA (USD million)	5,676	6,236	7,965	5,116	6,506	8,866	9,417	9,544	7,500	5,427	5,988
EBITDA adjusted (RUB million)	154,330	168,854	214,045	189,590	219,454	300,077	323,106	336,752	342,614	404,811	456,198
EBITDA adjusted (USD million)	6,093	6,601	8,610	5,977	7,226	9,806	9,972	10,155	8,544	6,365	6,790
Net income (RUB million)	99,543	105,978	115,798	95,572	95,605	167,669	184,152	186,720	126,656	116,198	209,725
Net income (USD million)	3,661	4,143	4,658	3,013	3,148	5,479	5,684	5,631	3,159	1,827	3,121
EBITDA margin	28.1	29.0	25.4	24.7	22.0	29.1	26.2	26.6	24.3	27.6	29.5
Net debt/EBITDA	0.0	0.3	0.0	1.1	0.9	0.7	0.5	0.6	1.4	1.9	1.6
Share price (RUB, at the end of the year)	119.9	151.74	62.67	163.64	128.27	148.18	142.52	146.77	143.00	153.95	214.0
Brent (USD/bbl)	65.14	72.3	97.3	61.7	79.5	111.3	111.7	108.7	98.9	52.5	43.7
Urals spot (USD/bbl)	61.28	69.2	94.8	61.2	78.3	109.1	110.4	107.7	96.9	51.5	42
Operating indicators											
Oil production (million tons)	44.4	43.1	46.3	47.6	49.6	50.0	50.8	50.6	52.1	55.7	59.8
Hydrocarbons production (MMtoe)	46.1	44.7	48.7	50.2	52.8	57.3	59.7	62.3	66.3	79.7	86.2
Refining throughput (million tons)	24.2	26.2	28.4	33.4	37.9	40.5	43.3	42.6	43.5	43.1	41.9
Number of employees	47,965	48,327	48,014	50,771	64,895	58,905	54,829	55,975	57,772	61,862	66,561

Source: Gazprom Neft Annual Reports

137

7

Herman Gref at Sberbank: Entrepreneurship in the Least Likely Place

I think I am difficult to satisfy, because when I win something, I'm already thinking about the next step, and that is maybe a problem for me. I'm not enjoying the moment. I'm already on the mission to win the next trophy.

– Zlatan Ibrahimovic

If I could be really good at other sports, I'd want to pitch to Barry Bonds, guard Michael Jordan, sidestep Ray Lewis, or stop Wayne Gretzky when they were at their best. I might not succeed, but I wouldn't want to spend my career training every day without measuring myself against the best.

– Michael Phelps

Herman Gref, the CEO of the Russia's largest bank, is probably the closest match to the model of the athletic leader among the protagonists of this book. The scale of his work is unprecedented. In less than ten years, he transformed a clumsy, old-fashioned, gigantic bank into one of the country's most innovative companies – a change that is visible to literally every Russian citizen.

Herman Gref: Profile of a Leader

In 2007, to the big surprise of the international financial community, the former minister of economic development and trade of the Russian Federation, Herman Gref, became the new CEO of Sberbank. At age 43, Gref had a spectacular government career behind him but had never worked in business. Born into a family of ethnic Germans in a small town in Northern Kazakhstan, he graduated from the prestigious St Petersburg University with a degree in economics and became engaged in social and political life during the perestroika years. After holding government jobs at district and city levels in St Petersburg, he went to Moscow to head a 'centre of strategy' that had been set up to create a blueprint for the economic development of Russia. There he assembled a team of experts from different spheres of life and engaged various organizations to contribute to the centre's work. The ideas thus developed formed the foundation of President Vladimir Putin's initial reforms in early 2000, which are recognized for having given a significant a boost to Russian economy. Gref then became a minister and earned a reputation as a committed liberal reformer who could push his agenda through the corridors of power. The media has credited him with many of the achievements of the early 2000s, such as the liberalization of taxation, the creation of Russia's Stabilization Fund, and entry into the World Trade Organization entry. Gref had worked with Putin when at the mayor's office of St Petersburg, so had direct access to the president. Many observers considered him a potential successor to Putin, but Gref decided to make a dramatic change and joined Sberbank.

However, he was an *outsider* in the banking industry. The Russian media met his appointment with scepticism, alluding to the 'lack of banking experience' and the 'romanticism' of the new CEO. Gref was undaunted. With his legendary work ethic – he puts in 16 hours a day – he dived into Sberbank. He had three goals at this stage: to become a banker, to build a team and to focus the organization's attention on performance.

Gref recalls, 'My motivation was simple: I wanted to demonstrate that a large state-owned Russian company could become world class.'[1] In the years that followed, nothing weakened his *belief in his ability to win*, whether it was the global financial crisis, Russia's economic slowdown or widespread geopolitical tensions.

---

[1] In interview with authors.

As Lev Khasis, his deputy, puts it, 'There is nothing impossible for Gref.' His *dissatisfaction with the status quo* is widely known. In 2015, just after completing the large-scale transformation of Sberbank's IT system, Gref announced that the new system was already outdated and needed reinvention. Alexander Torbakhov, head of retail operations, says, 'I've met a lot of outstanding people, but Gref is unique in terms of personality. It may sound both positive and negative!'[2]

Sberbank's CEO is not an easy boss to have. Not only does he work extremely hard and expect others to do the same but he is also very opinionated and does not always choose his words carefully. Gref is quick to criticize mistakes and views that he does not share, regardless of who expresses them, and he does not often praise subordinates. He is easily excited and tends to lose track of time, which ruins his own and his subordinates' schedules. Yet, as one of his deputies says, 'the thrill of what we are doing with him at Sberbank compensates for all of these inconveniences'.[3] The CEO also forces the members of his executive team to lead a healthy lifestyle, openly criticizing those whom he finds unfit or overweight. Gref himself runs five miles every morning.

Of all our athletic leaders, it is Gref who sets the bar *of developmental focus* highest – and at an almost unattainable level. He claims to have the 'complex of an uneducated man' and is working hard to deal with it. He has a passion for reading and highly respects scholars and experts, but he seeks knowledge from all possible sources – from front-line bank employees to CEOs of global companies. Gref is always on the lookout for new ideas and does not hesitate to try them out.

Teaching Sberbank to Rock and Roll

Sberbank (or 'Savings Bank of Russia') was established in 1841 by decree of Tsar Nikolay I. Throughout Soviet times Sberbank remained the sole provider of retail banking services in the country – every citizen with a bank account was its client. After

[2] In interview with authors.
[3] In interview with authors.

the USSR collapsed, the bank's operations in the territory of the Russian Federation were rebranded as Sberbank of Russia. Since 1996 it has been listed on the Moscow Stock Exchange.

By 2007, Sberbank had more than US$190 billion in assets, which made it the biggest bank in Eastern Europe and number 33 in the world. Its branch network consisted of 20,000 retail outlets across the country. With 262,000 people on its payroll, it was one of the largest employers in Russia – and in many parts of the country the only financial institution. Despite good financial results Sberbank remained a huge and clumsy machine, notorious for poor service, obsolescence and a Soviet mentality. It lagged behind not only leading international banks but also private Russian competitors in terms of productivity and efficiency.

In 2007, when the previous CEO, Andrey Kaz'min, moved on to head Russian Post, most senior executives left the bank as well. The new leader engaged an executive search company, Ward Howell, to help him assemble a team. Sergey Vorobiev, Ward Howell's senior partner, remembers, 'Gref wanted top talent – superprofessionals with supermotivation. We used to tell candidates that there are greenfield companies, brownfield companies [...] but Sberbank was a blackfield. We were looking for rebels.'[4]

The new team comprising people from leading international companies – Denis Bugrov (McKinsey), Anton Karamzin (Morgan Stanley) and Viktor Orlovsky (IBM) among others – was operational in early 2008. However, Gref never stopped searching for top talent both outside and inside Sberbank. In the following years, Alexander Bazarov (Deutsche Bank, Credit Suisse), Sergey Gorkov (Yukos) and Lev Khasis (Walmart, X5 Retail Group) joined the team from the market, while Maxim Poletaev and Alexander Morozov were promoted from within.

In September 2008, Sberbank unveiled its new five-year strategy. The ultimate goal was to become one of the world's leading financial institutions. The bank planned to increase after-tax profits by 250 per cent to 350 per cent, ensuring return on equity above 20 per cent, and to reduce headcount by 15 per cent to 20 per cent.

[4] In interview with authors.

The number one focus was operational efficiency, but Gref wanted to achieve this through learning and innovation rather than drastic cost cutting. In his first memo to Sberbank employees (a form of communication that would became a tradition), the CEO set the course for 260,000 people to embark on a voyage of change:

> Our competitors have learned to work more efficiently and much faster – they know the needs of their clients and react to them instantly. We need to remember the lessons from history – clumsy empires break down. Clients need change. Consumers today have a wide choice, and we need to change to preserve our leading position.[5]

Gref is a great fan of 'lean production', the management philosophy derived from the Toyota Production System, and he felt Sberbank was the right place to apply it. Under Gref's leadership the Sberbank Production System (SPS) was created. This covers different areas – process optimization, management system development (KPIs and incentives) and promotion of new values – and is continuously evolving. To introduce SPS to the bank on a large scale, Gref picked a manager with significant Sberbank experience: Maxim Poletaev, who was the youngest chairman of one of the regional banks at that time. Poletaev went to Cape Town to a lean production school and later led a large group of Sberbank executives on a visit to Toyota factories in Japan.

Two 'lean laboratories' were opened in Moscow and Nizhny Novgorod to educate staff, and, by 2012, 75,000 Sberbank employees had completed their training. Gref went on the course too – and received the highest qualification: a 'black belt'.

Lean production strives to identify and continuously eliminate ineffective and inefficient areas and processes. The visual symbol of inefficiency in Sberbank was always the length of customer queues. This became a top priority for Gref and his team. The first steps were quite simple: to abandon the daily closure of Sberbank retail offices for lunch by putting employees on flexible lunch breaks. More sophisticated measures followed later. A new

---

[5] 'A letter to each Sberbank' employee', *Sberbank internal document,* 1 July 2008.

IT system sorted customers based on their enquiries, give them information about the likely waiting time and monitored actual service time. The bank actively promoted such services as e-banking and direct debit to keep customers from visiting its offices with small queries. By 2012, queuing time had fallen by 35 per cent, personal efficiency of employees had risen by 25 percept and retail sales had multiplied by two and a half.

One of the key mechanisms for improving service quality was managing customer complaints and claims (like Saveliev, Gref loves *A Complaint Is a Gift: Recovering Customer Loyalty When Things Go Wrong* by Janelle Barlow). The entire complaints and claims process was built from scratch in a very short time and provided management with a great deal of data about areas for improvement. As one of Sberbank's employees says, 'Gref is constantly monitoring the complaint process; he can just pick up one case and push everyone to solve the problem.'[6] Alexander Torbakhov, head of retail network, explains, 'Gref is crazy about clients, what they really want and need. This is not up for debate.'[7] Another employee, who worked in the company long before Gref's appointment, describes the process of reforms:

> We had not anticipated such radical changes. The pressure was enormous. As a result, the culture of client service changed completely. At the same time, many people, good people, left because of the new management's high demands. I stayed only because I was curious what would happen next.[8]

To support the productivity of front-line employees, Sberbank took a hard look at its back office. The new management quickly understood that many policies and procedures made very little sense and directly destroyed value. They introduced the concept of shared services centres ('customer transaction support centres' in Sberbank terminology). The first two opened in Moscow and St Petersburg, and two more were eventually added (one of them becoming the biggest in Europe). These facilities allowed Sberbank to free front offices from payment transactions, the processing of credit requests,

[6] In interview with authors.
[7] In interview with authors.
[8] In interview with authors.

collection of bad debt, and hundreds of other operations. The overall economic effect was more than US$1 billion.

Gref believes that IT is a core enabling function of a modern bank. The scale of this operation at Sberbank is enormous. Gref has even described the organization as 'the biggest IT company in Russia'. The breakdown of Sberbank's IT platform could paralyze the whole banking system of Russia, while the failure of payment and deposit systems could result in a social earthquake (non-payment of pensions, welfare allocations, wages, etc.). In July of 2012, the company's card-processing system crashed nationwide. This lasted two hours and caused a media storm. 'Angry clients were calling in to live radio programmes. At the following management meeting I said that it was cool to be innovative but our first priority should be safety,'[9] recalls Torbakhov.

By 2015, Sberbank had completed its programme of centralizing IT systems, which was unprecedented in terms of speed and scale – and, the following year, won the international 'Model Bank' award for 'Legacy Transformation'. The company consolidated more than 2,500 regional technological platforms into one, reduced the number of support centres from 800 to 8, built data storage and, as a result, improved service, increased productivity (reducing headcount from 52,000 to 17,000) and significantly cut the amount of time required to deploy new banking products.

Unification of business processes and policies, and centralization of core functions had an immediate bottom-line impact. However, this came with some costs. For example, employees of regional subsidiaries felt disfranchised. According to one of them,

> Before Gref's appointment we felt the responsibility for the financial performance of our small office. The headquarters were too far away. The new [management] team brought them closer, but at the same time it took away our control over the situation and our pride for the job done.[10]

Sberbank had to overcome this mentality and make all employees feel a part of the one big company.

[9] In interview with authors.
[10] In interview with authors.

Building World-Class Human Capital: Competencies and Values

Gref and his team understood that it is not enough to change processes and procedures – a bank is about people: their skills, motivations and behaviours. As the CEO says,

> If we wanted to have a leading financial institution we needed to have a quality workforce and we did not. Even from the point of view of general education, we were at a disadvantage – most of our managers graduated from provincial colleges and did so at the worst possible time, the late 1980s and early 1990s, when our education system almost collapsed. We had to educate them.[11]

Gref believes that, in order to become a world-class bank, Sberbank needs to have a world-class corporate university – and the second must precede the first. He recruited Professor Valery Katkalo, dean of the Graduate School of Management at St Petersburg University (the only Russian business school to make it into the *Financial Times* top-100 list), to head Sberbank Corporate University. The bank invested more than 10 billion roubles (US$303 million) in refurbishing its numerous training facilities and building a state-of-the art campus just outside Moscow. The corporate university launched a number of customized management development programmes with leading international business schools – INSEAD, LBS and Stanford. The Sberbank–INSEAD programme, for example, is unprecedented – every year 500 high-potential managers attend a nine-month course, which combines traditional classroom learning with online sessions and group and individual projects. 'Self-development became our corporate DNA,'[12] comments Valery Katkalo. Sberbank remains a leader in corporate education. In 2015, it spent around 3.4 billion roubles (about US$56 million).

Gref is a great believer in management wisdom. He created a 'corporate library', which contains books that are 'necessary for our employees and managers' – not only business literature

---

[11] In interview with authors.
[12] In interview with authors.

but also books about improving personal relationships or health. Rumour has it that Gref reads them all and regularly tests other Sberbank employees on whether they do the same. Sberbank also invites international guest speakers from academia and business to lecture its managers, attracting audiences of up to 1,500 at a time. To reach out to its 325,000-strong workforce spread across 13 time zones Sberbank actively experiments with distance learning. In 2012, it launched a virtual school for employees with more than 300 multimedia courses, video lectures and iPad apps.

Constant thirst for knowledge has led the CEO and his team to look for innovative ways of acquiring it. One such innovation is a learning partnership with Boeing. Gref believes that the best learning comes from industries other than your own and that Sberbank can find out a great deal about developing talent, planning long term, using IT and managing organizational complexity from the American aircraft manufacturer. A large group of the bank's managers has been to Seattle to visit Boeing's headquarters and plants, while Boeing executives regularly lecture at Sberbank's conferences and retreats. Oleg Smirnov, who now runs the largest regional operation (Moscow), recalls, 'It was a very powerful trip [to Boeing]. I remember we asked a truck driver: "What do you do?" and he answered, "I build planes." I will not forget it.'[13]

Gref likes to repeat that he is the chief human resources officer at Sberbank. He might also claim to be the chief education officer. Not only has he promoted employee development through multi-million-dollar investments but he also actively participates in the development process. Gref talks to people on his numerous trips to the regions, speaks at all major management development programmes and, since 2008, has written 'letters to employees' and asked them to write back. He also pushes other executives to do the same. Every day members of the executive board send an email, 'Good morning, Sberbank!', motivating employees and giving simple advice on how to improve personal efficiency. Recently Gref introduced the concept of 'leaders teaching leaders', whereby each member of the management team (around 250 people) regularly engages in education at Sberbank as a teacher.

[13] In interview with authors.

Thanks to Gref's constant drive for knowledge and innovation, Sberbank is always on the move. As one ex-member of his team says, 'It was very hard to work at Sberbank – a lot of additional activities. You can't just do your job. They need to see your loyalty and passion, and it's not a place where everyone can survive.'[14] Gref is not shy about his values. He continuously preaches performance, development and a healthy lifestyle with both words and actions. His 'propaganda' works: thousands of Sberbank employees regularly participate in all types of sporting activities and have become devoted readers of management bestsellers. The HR department even runs a company-wide project to educate employees about healthy food and fitness.

Nevertheless, the CEO is deeply concerned about the bank's culture: 'With our investments in education we have provided people with the required skills, but can we create a productive culture in a country where it has never existed?' he asks. 'Without it, Sberbank will not make it to the top league,' he adds.[15] He constantly reflects on the subject, reads books, talks to experts and, of course, acts.

In 2009, Sberbank published its first mission statement: 'We give people confidence and security; we make people's lives better by helping them to fulfil their dreams and aspirations.' Later this was complemented by the goal 'to build one of the best financial companies in the world'. There is also a set of 'Sberbank Rules', which aims to help employees navigate their day-to-day activities, for example, 'Go beyond selling a product; build relationships', 'Follow the spirit, not just the letter of the law' and, perhaps the most important reflection of what is expected from employees, 'Improve yourself and your environment day by day.'

However, by 2013 Gref felt the need to take a hard new look at values and the corporate culture and to make this one of the principal drivers of the bank's development. Numerous conversations with external experts and among members of the management team led to a retreat, which produced a set of Sberbank values: 'I am a leader', 'We are a team' and 'Everything

[14] In interview with authors.
[15] In interview with authors.

for the customer.' According to surveys, focus groups and crowdsourcing initiatives, the new values resonated well with the bank's employees, who in general believed that leadership and customer orientation had already become true organizational values, while teamwork was greatly needed and appreciated but not yet embedded in the collective corporate subconscious. Gref did not stop there, though. He hired Julia Chupina, another ex-McKinsey star and ex-vice president at rival bank VTB, as a special adviser to oversee corporate culture.

Gref argues that different cultures can coexist within Sberbank. In 2016, he told *Harvard Business Review Russia,*

> Inside one company we should combine three completely different cultures. The first – accuracy and elimination of mistakes. The second – speed and risk in changing technological platforms, but without fatal mistakes. And the third – simplicity, creativity and t-shirts with the slogan 'I love failure'. It is critical not to mix up these cultures.[16]

Teaching Sberbank to Fly

By 2016, Sberbank had changed significantly. That year it showed the largest net profit in its 175-year history (542 billion roubles or US$8 billion; see Table 7.1) and, for the first time, became the largest Russian company by market capitalization (overtaking Gazprom and Rosneft). By now Sberbank had 146 million customers in 22 countries, over 47 million active users of its online bank and over 20 million active users of its mobile apps. Sberbank's brand value was estimated at US$9.1 billion – the sixth highest among European banks and twenty-fourth among global banks (according to Brand Finance).

However, according to Gref, Sberbank's main competitors were no longer banks. Speaking at an annual shareholder meeting in June 2014 (wearing a Google Glass headset), Gref described the bank's future: 'We will not compete with traditional banks, we will compete with modern, fast, huge internet platforms such

[16] M. Ivanyushchenkova, 'Herman Gref: "Russian Management Style Is Not Efficient, But Effective"', *Harvard Business Review Russia*, 26 January 2016.

as Google, Amazon, etc.' He also cited Bill Gates: 'Banking is necessary – banks are not.'[17]

In recognition of the major threat posed by non-banking organizations, Sberbank invests in the financial industry's most promising start-ups, thanks to the creation in 2012 of Sberbank Venture Capital. By 2015 this fund had invested around US$40 million in 11 companies, among them GridGain (a provider of enterprise-grade, in-memory computing solutions for high-volume transactions, real-time analytics and hybrid data processing) and Platius (the developer of a loyalty and mobile payment system with ambitions to roll out nationwide). According to Lev Khasis, Sberbank 'plans to create a fintech ecosystem, built around the interests of the client'.[18]

In March of 2016, Gref and his team visited Stanford University as part of an annual executive education programme for Sberbank's CEO and his direct reports. There they met with leading technology businesses and start-ups. Gref was impressed by how fast these companies were able to move – developing and launching new products in days rather than months or years. He returned to Moscow inspired to make Sberbank equally fast and innovative and gave a lecture to employees, stating, 'There is no competition among products or services; there is only competition between management systems.'[19] He then announced 'probably the most radical transformation in our bank's 175-year history' based on deployment of the 'Agile' management system. The process came to be known as *Sbergile*. During 2016, 125 'agile' teams (more than 1,000 employees) started their work in a new office building designed according to agile principles. Sberbank has committed that all of the company's corporate and retail businesses will be working in agile format by the end of 2017. Lev Khasis told the media,

> By implementing the Agile methodology, we are bringing new products to market more quickly. In the next two years, we will move to a fundamentally new technological platform, where our

[17] Herman Gref's speech, *Sberbank' Annual Shareholders Meeting*, 26 May 2017.
[18] In interview with authors.
[19] Herman Gref's speech, *Sberbank's Leaders Meeting*, 15 March 2016.

clients will be able to receive not only our services but also the services of our partners.[20]

Making Sberbank agile is not an easy ride. Some people make fun of an unknown English word and intentionally distort it. Others complain about the pace of change. One employee told us,

> People are tired of change. Every week you are told that 'it will be a new organization structure soon, some of you will probably lose your jobs'. I understand that the company needs to move and to change, but people can't change every week. They need stability.[21]

By 2015, Sberbank had finished the unification of its IT system, but – to everyone's surprise – Gref admitted to the media, 'The moment we completed it, we understood that what we had created was compatible with banks but not technological companies.'[22] Sberbank started completely redesigning its IT system all over again, based on the principles of cloud services, open source and in-memory computing. The portfolio of IT projects grew significantly. In 2015, Sberbank Technologies, the IT division, received contracts from the rest of the company worth more than 16 billion roubles.

As the backbone of Russia's financial system, Sberbank has access to enormous amounts of data about how people all over the country earn, save and spend money. In 2016, the company launched its 'Open Data' project, a website where everyone can get information about consumers' financial behaviour across all Russian regions. Other companies can also buy more detailed data from Sberbank. The company also launched an artificial intelligence project called IPavlov, aimed at developing new business applications. This will be fully integrated into the bank's work and allow it to take client services to a new level. Gref told *Harvard Business Review Russia*, 'Today our business is all about technologies. We've started to use big data, machine learning,

---

[20] Lev Khasis's speech, Sibos 2016 Forum, 26 September 2016.
[21] In interview with authors.
[22] S. Sharoyan, 'Gref Considered Sberbank' Billion-Rouble IT-system to Be Outdated', *RBK*, 15 January, 2016.

artificial intelligence, making billions (of dollars using these technologies).'[23]

In 2016, consulting company Deloitte put Sberbank on top of its list of the most innovative Russian banks. Experts chose a dozen of the most important innovations, such as biometric identification, digital wallets, non-contact technologies and big data. According to the research, eight of Sberbank's new services are unique in the market. To assess whether clients are ready to use these innovations, Sberbank launched the Digital Ivanov Index, designed to evaluate the level of penetration of digital technology in Russia. The index was based on five factors: Internet access, human capital, Internet use, e-commerce and banking, and e-government. The first Digital Ivanov Index score was 51 per cent. Sberbank interpreted this figure to mean that digital development had reached a 'tipping point'. That is, many people in Russia use technology and are computer literate, but there is still great potential for growth. Sberbank is ready to boost this growth together with the government. 'It is impossible to be successful if you don't connect your services with government services. That's why we are working together to build new digital strategy,'[24] Gref told the World Economic Forum.

During the same session in Davos, Gref confided that the number one threat to innovation is overregulation. He used the story of blockchain development (he is a great supporter of this technology and a bitcoin investor) as an illustration:

> If you speak with central banks about virtual currency, they try to regulate it immediately. I beg your pardon, could you take a little bit more time to understand what kind of outputs we can get from these technologies? And when these technologies are mature you can regulate them but not before![25]

The relationship between the Russian government and Sberbank has never been simple. As the backbone of the Russian financial

---

[23] Ivanyushchenkova, 'Herman Gref: "Russian Management Style"'.

[24] Interview with Kaiser Kuo, *World Economic Forum* session 'Shaping a National Digital Strategy', January 2017.

[25] Ibid.

system, the company is under the strict control of its main shareholder, Central Bank of Russia, which owns 52.32 per cent of Sberbank shares, and the Russian government. Sberbank is also the largest taxpayer in the majority of Russian regions. Gref regularly meets with President Putin and updates him on Sberbank and the whole banking industry's performance. The bank is instrumental in carrying out many government economic policies and initiatives, such as subsidizing the development of Russian agriculture or small businesses. The Sberbank CEO constantly gets requests for help from ministers, heads of government agencies and leaders and owners of state-owned and private companies. He has to perform a tough balancing act, protecting the interests of his public shareholders and maintaining favourable relationships with the country's key people and institutions.

Gref's government experience helps him get along with different government bodies, especially Russia's central bank. He told Russian business daily *Vedomosti*,

> There are a lot of changes, [reserve] requirements have risen sharply, which takes a heavy toll on banks' equity. It forces us to seriously change internal procedures [...] Banks are grumbling about this and I would grumble too if we did not work in many markets. We see how regulators operate in Europe, Turkey, or the USA. After seeing them I cannot say that our regulator is too tough.[26]

Despite being highly dependent on relationships with government, Gref has gained the reputation of a straight-talker who is not afraid to speak out about economic and political problems. However, he never criticizes specific people, only the government as a whole or the *sistema*, a Russian euphemism for the networks-based system of governance. Speaking at the Gaidar Economic Forum in 2016, Gref shocked the audience by saying, 'We [Russia] lost the competition and now we are among the declining countries. What do we need to do? We need to change all government institutions.'[27] Gref

---

[26] T. Voronova, F. Sterkin and D. Borisyak, 'Today We Have Perfect Conditions for Reforms', *Vedomosti*, 27 December 2016.

[27] Herman Gref's speech, *Gaidar Forum*, 1 January 2016.

showed once again that this is not just talk – Sberbank Corporate University has started seminars for senior government officials to enlighten them on recent leadership and management thinking. As one of Sberbank's employees told us, 'Herman Gref is a state man. I'm proud that our CEO is brave enough not to change only Sberbank.' However, the same employee also confided, 'Inside Sberbank, it looks like a Gref personality cult. It's over the top.'[28]

Gref's ambitious plans are influenced by a number of negative factors, including falling oil prices, geopolitical tensions, subsequent sanctions against Russia and overall economic slowdown. In 2015, Sberbank had to update its strategy for 2014–18, decreasing key targets. As Gref told *Harvard Business Review Russia*,

> Under conditions of greater uncertainty you should move on 'soft legs'. When you are skiing and the mist is coming, you bend your legs. Because at great speed, in zero visibility and with straight legs, you will get injured. It's the same in business – you need to be flexible, give people the right to make mistakes, and create tools that enable employees to be more creative – and to tell the truth to each other.[29]

Yet in 2016 Sberbank demonstrated record profits, strengthened its position as a market leader in customer service and innovation and its stock skyrocketed. Gref presses ahead with his digital transformation agenda. He hired Bart Schlatmann, who led an agile transformation of ING Netherlands, as a chief digital transformation officer. Sberbank opened a separate Agile-office in downtown Moscow to host thousands of employees working in new conditions, developing new products for the customers and systems for the bank. In 2016, a new product entered the market every month, the target for 2017 – to present innovations on a weekly basis. In Sberbank's pipeline there are such services as face recognition at ATMs and online 'Sber wrist-bracelets' to monitor body conditions, walking distance and to make payments; loans to individuals not buying but selling used cars; and Sberbank's virtual mobile operator. As always, the CEO is enthusiastic and realistic

---

[28] In interview with authors.
[29] Ivanyushchenkova, 'Herman Gref: "Russian Management Style"'.

at the same time: 'We are living through the most profound and prolonged crisis in the last 20 years, but we know how to navigate it better than others and we will keep pleasantly surprising our customers and shareholders.'[30] We are confident Gref will keep surprising Sberbank employees and competitors as well.

[30] Herman Gref's speech, *Sberbank' Annual Shareholders Meeting*, 26 May 2017.

Table 7.1 Sberbank Performance (2007–16)

	2007	2008	2009	2010	2011	2012	2013	2014	2015	2016
Financial indicators										
Assets (USD million)	192,651	270,958	223,217	284,222	368,662	485,746	571,742	652,710	448,850	337,380
Assets (RUB billion)	4,928	6,736	7,097	8,628	10,835	15,097	18,210	25,201	27,335	25,352
Liabilities (USD million)	167,788	240,789	184,165	203,952	285,199	355,984	425,243	600,380	409,850	335,550
Liabilities (RUB billion)	4,292	5,986	6,248	7,641	9,567	9,118	11,930	23,181	24,960	22,542
Total client deposits (USD million)	151,588	192,889	170,874	219,072	269,888	327,510	378,776	403,083	325,091	278,131
Total client deposits (RUB billion)	3,878	4,795	5,439	6,651	7,932	10,179	12,064	15,563	19,798	18,685
Net profit (USD million)	4,164	3,930	766	5,981	10,748	11,193	11,365	7,520	3,660	8,070
Net profit (RUB billion)	106.5	97.7	24.4	181.6	315.9	347.9	362.0	290.3	222.9	541.9
Operating income before provisions (USD million)	13,804	14,152	20,362	21,404	25,053	29,627	34,657	33,689	23,478	25,268
Operating income before provisions (RUB billion)	353	352	648	650	736	921	1,104	1,301	1,430	1,698

Earnings per ordinary share (USD)	0.2	0.18	0.03	0.27	0.49	0.51	0.52	0.35	0.16	0.41
Earnings per ordinary share (RUB)	5.1	4.5	1.1	8.42	14.61	16.03	16.78	13.45	10.36	25.0
Operating indicators										
Share assets (%)	25	24.7	26.2	27.3	26.8	28.9	29.6	29.1	28.7	28.9
Share of the retail deposit market (%)	51.4	51.9	49.4	47.9	46.6	45.7	46.7	45.0	46.0	46.6
Share of the corporate deposit market (%)	17.9	17.7	20.6	15.9	14.5	17.2	17.2	21.9	25.0	22.1
Share of the retail loan market (%)	32.1	31.3	32.7	31.9	32.0	32.7	33.5	35.9	38.7	40.1
Share of the corporate loan market (%)	32.7	30.5	31.8	31.3	32.9	33.6	33.3	35.0	32.2	31.7
Number of employees (thousand)	262.4	270.0	249.8	237.2	231.3	233.3	255.5	275.7	330.7	325.1

Source: Sberbank Annual Reports

8

Athletic Leadership in Other Regions: Roger Agnelli, Dong Mingzhu and Jeff Bezos

Success is no accident. It is hard work, perseverance, learning, studying, sacrifice and most of all, love of what you are doing or learning to do.

– Pele

If you don't have confidence, you'll always find a way not to win.

– Carl Lewis

As demonstrated in the previous chapters, athletic leaders can be extremely successful in turbulent, government-dominated environments with rapid knowledge obsolescence – conditions that are met in contexts other than Russia. In search of non-Russian athletic leaders, we first took a look at the BRICS (Brazil, Russia, India, China and South Africa). We tried to identify companies that had achieved world-beating status and examined whether their CEOs possessed the attributes of athletic leaders. We were especially interested in finding a woman CEO to test our hypothesis that, even though athletic leadership may seem quite *masculine*, it is independent of gender and can be successfully practiced by female executives.

What if athletic leadership could be effective in developed economies too? Rapid change and knowledge obsolescence, turbulence and heavy government interference need not be characteristics of the market as a whole but of a specific industry, such as technology. If you were asked to name the greatest business leader in this sector, you would probably say Steve Jobs, Elon Musk, Bill Gates or Jeff Bezos – all of them from technology companies, all of them from one of the world's most developed markets (the United States), all of them quite different from the identikit portraits painted by the leadership literature and all of them bearing a striking resemblance to athletic leaders.

In this chapter, we focus on three athletic leaders from different parts of the world: Roger Agnelli, former CEO of Brazilian Vale; Dong Minzhu, CEO of Chinese Gree Electric; and Jeff Bezos, president, CEO and chairman of United States-based Amazon. All three not only exemplify the mindset of athletic leaders (mental toughness, adaptability, super-sized ambition etc.) but have also used the same metapractices in defining their company's path, obtaining new knowledge and dealing with followers, media and government.

Brazil: Roger Agnelli

A member of the BRICS, Brazil is one of the major emerging economies and the seventh largest in the world, with GDP of 3.2 trillion international dollars (PPP) in 2016. After struggling with severe inflation at the beginning of the 1990s, Brazil's government in 1994 introduced the 'Real Plan' in an attempt to stabilize the economy through the introduction of a new currency – the real. This step successfully ended decades of macroeconomic uncertainty. Between 2003 and 2014, the country's GDP rose by an average of 4 per cent a year (thanks largely to a surge in prices of exported commodities), which resulted in significant economic and social progress. The government still dominates many areas of Brazil's economy: total government spending constitutes more than 40 per cent of GDP. However, in several waves of privatization, the Brazilian government has sold part of its stake in the country's largest enterprises, including Vale.

Vale (known as CVRD before its rebranding in 2007) was founded in 1942 by the Brazilian federal government and, by the middle of the 1970s, had become the world's largest exporter of iron ore. In 1997, despite widespread criticism, 41.7 per cent of

Vale's shares were privatized, with Bradesco becoming the leading investor. Representing Bradesco in this complex transaction was a 38-year-old investment banker called Roger Agnelli. Three years later, he made a successful bid to become Vale's chairman and in 2001 took over as CEO.

What happened during the next 10 years of Agnelli's tenure has become one of the greatest business stories of all time: Vale transformed itself from being a primarily Brazilian-focused exporter into a truly global company with operations in more than 38 countries. The company's revenues grew from US$4 billion in 2001 to US$60 billion in 2011; its net profit increased from US$1 billion to US$23 billion; and its staff numbers swelled from 11,000 to 190,000. Today, Vale is the world's largest iron ore and nickel producer, and one of the leaders in its field in terms of phosphates, nitrogen, copper and manganese minerals.

Vale has not only demonstrated outstanding financial performance but has also revolutionized Brazil's mining industry, investing heavily in new technologies and building non-traditional mines, which have been successfully incorporated into local communities. The company has also revamped the nation's railroad sector and shipping industry, creating a new system of transportation and communication networks. Vale has earned international recognition for its sustainable development programmes, which preserve ecosystems and support education, community health and sanitation projects throughout Brazil and beyond (especially in Africa).

In a ranking of the world's best-performing CEOs published in *Harvard Business Review* in February 2013, Agnelli came in fourth – behind only Apple's Steve Jobs, Amazon's Jeff Bezos, and Yun Jong-Yong of Samsung Group. The researchers greatly praised Vale's increased market capitalization of US$157 billion (up from US$9.2 billion in 2001) and total shareholder return of 934 per cent (adjusted for country) or 1,773 per cent (adjusted for industry) during Agnelli's tenure (2001 to 2011).

Roger Agnelli was born in São Paulo to a middle-class family of Italian origin in 1959. After graduation, he began his career in the banking industry, quickly gaining a reputation as a prodigy. At the age of 29, he became the youngest senior vice-president in Brazil's largest private bank, Bradesco, which changed its own policy in 1998 in order to appoint the 33-year-old Agnelli as general manager of the capital markets unit. Just three years later, he was CEO of Vale.

In an interview, Agnelli recounted how, at the beginning of his tenure, he met the CEO of one of the world's leading mining companies, who told him that he would like to buy Vale. Agnelli responded, 'Let's have this conversation in four years. Maybe we can talk then as equals. Or perhaps we will buy *your* company.'[1] As Agnelli had predicted, by the time of their next meeting, Vale was already the larger company. In 2002, he went on to decline a merger offer from Anglo-American. Refusing to listen to the critics, he was convinced that he was capable of building a global player.

While still working in investment banking, Agnelli had gained a reputation for having a nose for a good deal and outstanding negotiating skills. At Vale, these skills came in handy. Agnelli made deals that he considered ambitious but others called impudent. He bought companies in the Americas, Norway, Africa and China, and entered partnerships with ThyssenKrupp Stahl and various Australian mining companies. In 2006, Vale bought the Canadian nickel miner Inco for US$17.6 billion, at the time, the largest acquisition ever made by a Latin American company. In 2008, it announced a bid for the Anglo-Swiss mining giant Xstrata, a global player in nickel, copper and coal. The deal was cancelled, but the fact that Agnelli was striving for an acquisition of this magnitude in the first place was proof of his appetite for bold moves.

Sceptics said that Vale's success was a direct consequence of the boom in commodity prices (the price of iron ore had spiralled from US$50/tonne in 2008 to US$190/tonne in 2011). However, Agnelli responded in an interview, 'Just luck is not enough. My father always said, "Pray to Our Lady and do not run behind to see what happens." I pray to Our Lady, to whom I am devout, and she helps. But I also run a lot behind my goals.'[2]

---

[1] A. van Agtmael, *The Emerging Markets Century: How a New Breed of World-Class Companies Is Overtaking the World* (London: Free Press, 2007), p. 201.

[2] D. Friedlander, 'É hora de medidas de exceção', *O Estadao de S.Paulo*, 13 December 2008.

Agnelli was famous for his brash style, which seemed to be simultaneously confusing and convincing. He could passionately strive for a deal but at the same time never lost his head. One co-worker remarked, 'He is a brilliant negotiator who knows how to achieve what he wants, but he knows where to stop.'[3] Despite his audacity, Agnelli could pass on a good deal if its conditions exceeded his idea of prudence. No one ever saw him angry. He was also a workaholic. Vale once estimated that its CEO spent 800 hours a year on airplanes. Nevertheless, Agnelli tried not to miss football at the weekends or yacht races on his estate.

One of Agnelli's most important decisions was to focus on metals and related minerals, while selling businesses with no connection to the mining industry (e.g. pulp and paper). His goal was to build a global powerhouse – a 'one-stop shop' for the steel industry. Diversifying the product portfolio by adding other minerals and metals gave him enough room for manoeuvre but kept the company within well-defined borders.

Despite a significant improvement in miners' working and living conditions, Agnelli was under fire from the media and labour unions because of the company's international expansion. The unions insisted that Vale should invest more in creating jobs in Brazil. In the midst of a financial crisis, Agnelli fired 2,000 workers, resulting in a clash with Brazil's ruling Workers' Party. In an interview, he commented, 'I get paid to produce results, and the results are there, aren't they?'[4] Later, he added, 'Look, we're living in an exceptional situation. To deal with it, we must take exceptional measures.'

Agnelli confirmed that being a prodigy in investment banking had given him the opportunity to ask a lot of questions without fear of looking stupid: 'I learned it could be useful to ask a lot of "silly" questions.'[5] He continued to ask 'silly questions' at Vale whenever he did not understand something about the mining industry – and some of these questions challenged the realities of the business. Agnelli pitched a pragmatic exploration

---

[3] A. Khalip, 'Vale's Agnelli, from Prodigy Banker to Mining King,' *Reuters*, 14 March 2008.

[4] Friedlander, 'É hora de medidas de exceção'.

[5] Ibid.

approach: 'The mining business was very traditional and closed to new ideas. Globalization pushes companies to be more efficient. The answer I used to get before I took over was, "we are studying this issue". As an investment banker, I was used to asking for results, as opposed to more studies.'[6]

Agnelli commissioned a large-scale executive education programme from Massachusetts Institute of Technology (MIT) – and more than 400 of Vale's managers completed the course, which had three main learning streams: strategic global thinking, results-based decision making and interpersonal leadership in a diverse environment.

After his dismissal, Agnelli would return to MIT for 40 days of individual lessons on bioenergy and renewable energies – focusing on the genetic modification of sugarcane for the production of biomass to fuel airplanes.

With his movie-star looks, Agnelli always hogged the limelight wherever he went. Several former top managers at Vale said he would annihilate anyone who started to compete for attention.[7] He also liked extravagant gestures. When Dilma Rousseff became Brazil's president in January 2011, Agnelli – who was having troubles with the ruling Workers' Party – began to send flowers to the president's office every day. Rousseff had no sympathy for him and politely asked him to stop. Just a few months later, Agnelli was dismissed from Vale and later attended an award ceremony for Rousseff in New York. At the end of her speech, he tore a flower from an arrangement in the auditorium and handed it to her.[8]

Agnelli's dismissal was the result of his difficult relationship with the government, which still had a significant influence over the company through the indirect stakes held by state pension funds. On the one hand, Agnelli had fulfilled his remit of paying dividends and meeting social responsibilities. On the other hand, the leftist government disliked his strategy of expanding abroad. In 2007, left-wing politicians had even started a campaign called 'Vale Is Ours', blaming Agnelli for not creating enough jobs in Brazil

[6] L. Casanova, *Global Latinas: Latin America's Emerging Multinationals* (New York: Palgrave Macmillan, 2009), p. 34.
[7] R. Paduan, 'Vida nova para Roger Agnelli', *Exame.com*, 28 December 2011.
[8] Ibid.

and for buying cargo ships overseas. Agnelli finally succeeded in getting along with President Luiz Inácio Lula da Silva. During the financial crisis, he even secured a temporary easing of labour laws and agreed to give up his own salary. However, Lula's successor, Rousseff, soon replaced him with long-time Vale executive Murilo Ferreira, who was friendlier to the Workers' Party and to the new president in particular.

We mentioned in an earlier chapter that one of the main problems with athletic leaders is the issue of their leaving. It seems that this was a difficult period for Agnelli, but he quickly adapted to the new situation. He joked that he had thought about his next steps just an hour after walking out of Vale and decided to establish his own investment fund. He commented in an interview about his new way of life: 'Today, I have to adapt to a new reality. The agenda today is what I do. I go where I want, when I want and how I want. I am more of a mentor, a counselor, than an executive focused on the day to day. I'm in this process of adaptation because my characteristic is to get involved in everything.'[9]

In 2016, Agnelli, his wife and their two children died in a plane crash. 'We have lost a Brazilian of extraordinary entrepreneurial vision,' said President Rousseff in an official statement.

China: Dong Mingzhu

When discussing turbulent, government-influenced environments with strong cultural leadership traditions, it is impossible to overlook China, a country that has achieved one of the fastest transformations in history. Behind these changes stand leaders who are not very familiar to the Western public. Who are they and how have they turned their companies into truly global businesses?

One of the most striking characteristics of the Chinese business environment is the high proportion of women among its executives. On the one hand, this may be the result of a communist government policy that has *supported* women going out to work so as to increase the country's overall output. On the other hand, it could be a consequence of China's one-child policy, which *allows*

[9] R. Viturino, 'Roger Agnelli: Today Africa Looks Like China from the 1990s', *Epoca Negocios*, 28 January 2014.

women to go out to work by providing multiple grandparents to look after a single child. Research shows that women hold the CEO position in 4.5 per cent of Chinese-listed companies[10] – and this percentage is on the rise.

Female CEOs and entrepreneurs have become icons in China, and their stories are well known. In 2013, Chinese television launched a new television series called *Regretless Pursuit*, which told the tale of a girl, the youngest of seven children, born into a low-class family in Nanjing. She worked in a research institute until her husband died, leaving her a widow with a young son at the age of just 32. Today, this woman, Dong Mingzhu, or 'Sister Dong' as she is known, is ranked number one in the *Forbes* list of the 100 Top Businesswomen in China, and she has figured in numerous rankings of the most powerful women in the world.

In 1990, in search of a better job, the recently widowed Dong moved to the south of China. There she was hired as a salesperson by a small state-owned enterprise called Gree Electric, which produced air conditioners. Sent by her new employer to a poor province, she achieved outstanding results, accounting for one-eighth of the company's annual sales. Four years later, Dong became head of the sales department and immediately began to fight against deeply rooted practices such as deferred payments and excessive bonuses. During her first year in the job, there was a sevenfold increase in sales revenue, and Gree Electric became the leader in the Chinese market for air conditioners in terms of production and sales volume.

In 2001, Dong became CEO of the company and in 2012 its chair. Under her leadership, an unknown factory in the south of China, which had been producing only 20,000 air conditioners per year with annual revenues of around RMB20 million (US$5.6 million), became one of the world's largest household appliances company. Currently, Gree Electric has ten production facilities across China, Brazil and Pakistan – and an annual turnover of more than RMB100 billion (US$14 billion).

---

[10] K. Lam, P. McGuinness and J. P. Vieito, 'An Empirical Assessment of CEO Gender, Executive Compensation and Firm Performance in Chinese-Listed Enterprises', *Pacific-Basin Finance Journal* 21 (2013): 1136–59.

Soon after being promoted to the position of CEO, Dong set an ambitious goal 'to build a centenary enterprise'. However, this did not mean that she wanted the company to grow gradually. In 2005, Gree Electric's sales volume exceeded 10 million sets, making the company the largest air conditioner manufacturer in the world.

At that point, Dong decided to diversify Gree Electric's portfolio to include smart home appliances that could connect to the Internet, and later the company began to develop smart-phones that could manage all smart home appliances, with robotic equipment for logistics. Gree had invested heavily invested in R&D, establishing 52 research institutions and 632 advanced laboratories. It also acquired Yinlong Energy, a Zhuhai-based power supplier and manufacturer of batteries and electric vehicles, to support the production of solar-powered air conditioners. Dong insisted that such diversification made sense: 'If you blindly base your decision to diversify or not to diversify into one sector simply on how lucrative it is, the chances are it is not likely to succeed. At Gree, we always stick to specialized development. We have core technology and we fill in the gaps in the industry. We keep the legacy of specialization while we pursue diversification.'[11]

As far as Gree Electric's future is concerned, Dong is sure that 'there is no mountain that we cannot conquer. It is all about confidence.'[12] Her subordinates confirm, 'We never dare to say that something is impossible in front of her.'[13] For her part, Dong Mingzhu has promised not to retire until Gree Electric achieves revenue of RMB200 billion.

As Dong sees it, one of Gree Electric's main goals is to 'help the world better understand China'.[14] She believes that Chinese brands are underestimated throughout the world and is determined to rectify the situation. There is one story about a partner from the Middle East who wanted to place a big order with Gree Electric

[11] Dong Mingzhu of Gree Electric Applicances Inc. of Zhuhai. PwC's 18th Annual Global CEO Survey.
[12] C. Coonan, 'The House That Sister Dong Built', *The National*, 11 February 2010.
[13] P. Foster, 'Gree Electric's Dong Mingzhu: Why China's Leading Businesswoman Doesn't Do Holidays', *The Telegraph*, 24 August 2009.
[14] D. Ren, 'Succeeding by Degrees', *South China Morning Post*, 23 December 2013.

on condition that production would take place at a local plant so as to avoid 'Made in China' stickers. However, the deeply insulted Dong refused, insisting, 'Products made by the Chinese are by no means low quality.'[15]

Dong Mingzhu is sure that without her intense focus on the company, neither she nor Gree Electric would achieve success: 'For instance, I like to climb mountains and I like singing, but these are not going to help solve the company's problems, so you have to make a choice if you want to be successful and give up some personal interests.'[16] Her passion for work is famous: she has never taken a day off in almost 20 years. 'Sometimes, you have to make a choice: is your health more important to you, or your career?' she once said.[17]

In the 1990s, the Chinese air conditioning industry fell on hard times. There were too many companies producing too many different products, and they had to reduce prices constantly just to stay afloat. As head of sales, Dong convinced the CEO not to engage in price wars and to focus on quality instead: 'Competitors have never concerned me. My interest is markets and market needs. We need to focus on what customers want.'[18] Almost every year, she had to stand firm while all the sales managers appealed for lower prices. In 2001, a powerful retailer demanded that the company reduce its prices in order to keep its products on the shelves. Dong refused and started to build her own distribution network, known as the 'Gree Model' and based on a win-win rebate system. This became one of the most successful and innovative business practices in China. As a result, that year's sales figures showed a 38 per cent increase with no squeeze on profit margins.

Gree Electric likes to make disruptive changes. In 2005, it began offering a six-year free after-sales service for residential air conditioners (the world's longest standard warranty at that time), followed by a two-year free replacement. In both cases, it was a bombshell for competitors. Dong explained, 'When you

[15] Ibid.
[16] Coonan, 'The House That Sister Dong Built'.
[17] Coonan, 'The House That Sister Dong Built'.
[18] Dong Mingzhu of Gree Electric Appliances Inc. of Zhuhai. PwC's 18th Annual Global CEO Survey.

make promises, you need to follow through. You must offer good service. And quality. And then trust follows naturally.'[19]

Dubbed 'one of the toughest businesswomen in China' by the *New York Times*, Dong Mingzhu refused in her autobiography to apologize for her intensity and focus, recalling difficult moments throughout her life that had forced her to take strong action: 'I didn't want other people's sympathy, I just wanted to live a better life by relying on my own efforts. I always wanted to do my job perfectly.'[20]

'Where sister Dong walks, no grass grows' is a popular saying in the Chinese media[21] – and it is supported by many anecdotes. For example, the agent with the largest yearly sales – more than US$20 million (almost one-tenth of the company total) – once came to Dong's office and arrogantly asked for preferential treatment. She fired him on the spot. Later, she explained to the CEO, 'We should develop our marketing network according to a system, not just one or two able men.'[22]

Rumour has it that Dong once refused her own brother a discount when he asked for preferential treatment in running a Gree Electric dealership. After that, they did not speak for many years.[23] She also gave up the practice of inviting regional sales agents to dinners, sharing cold meals with them in a cafeteria instead. And she always goes on business trips alone: 'The principle is simple. If you take another person on a trip, you have to spend twice as much.'[24]

Despite her harsh management style, Dong does not try to demonstrate power through her appearance and always looks very feminine: 'Why should I wear a suit? I like wearing beautiful clothes.'[25]

The global financial crisis of 2008–9 hit the air conditioning industry hard. Nevertheless, Dong decided that this was the best

[19] D. Tatlow, 'Setting the Pace with Toughness', *New York Times*, 26 January 2011.
[20] Ibid.
[21] Ibid.
[22] 'Gree's Dong Mingzhu: A Career Woman Full of Great Ideas', *Chief Executive Magazine*. Translated by Women of China.
[23] Foster, 'Gree Electric's Dong Mingzhu'.
[24] 'Gree's Dong Mingzhu: A Career Woman Full of Great Ideas'.
[25] Ibid.

time for the company to expand: 'This financial crisis is a moment for Gree Electric to re-orientate itself. It is a golden chance for overseas customers to recognize that they can pay less for the best quality machines.'[26] In the midst of the crisis, while competitors were frantically trying to sell all of their stock, Gree Electric invested around RMB2 billion (US$289 million) in R&D. As a result, in 2008 growth slowed (a 10 per cent increase, compared to 44 per cent the previous year), but profits rose by 50 per cent.

Gree Electric is a public company, mostly controlled by the local government of Zhuhai City in Guangdong province. Dong is quite active in political life: she is a member of the China Democratic National Construction Association (one of the eight legally recognized Chinese political parties), and was formerly a member of three National People's Congresses. In addition, she holds several positions in a dozen industry bodies, women's organizations and charities, and has taught business classes at a university.

Gree Electric, as a state-owned company, receives some benefits from the government, such as a government-sponsored plan to deliver electrical goods to the countryside at a substantial discount. However, Dong does not consider this unusual: 'This company can't depend on government orders to stay competitive. We have to stay in front on quality and service. Many countries have stimulus packages. China is no different.'[27]

In November 2016, Gree Group removed Dong Mingzhu from the position of chair, but she stayed on as CEO of Gree Electric – a decision initiated by the main shareholder, Zhuhai City. The City Commission explained that it was normal practice that a chairperson could not simultaneously be an executive at one of the subsidiaries. At the same time, a leaked video from a Gree Group shareholders' meeting revealed strong opposition to Dong's bold acquisition programme, including a US$1.9 billion takeover of the electric carmaker Yinlong New Energy. There were also calls for the issuance of nearly a quarter of Gree Group's current total shares in private placement, which could cause significant dilution for the remaining shareholders. Dong

---

[26] Foster, 'Gree Electric's Dong Mingzhu'.
[27] Ibid.

exclaimed in a video, 'Sell the stocks all you want if you don't trust Gree, but if you do, trust firmly.'[28]

United States: Jeff Bezos

In 2012, Jeff Bezos appeared on the cover of *Forbes* magazine's issue on 'America's Best Leaders'. Two years later, he was ranked first in *Harvard Business Review*'s 'Best Performing CEOs in the World'. So what type of leader is Bezos? Our research shows that he has all the attributes of an athletic leader: mental toughness, adaptability and a strong leadership narrative. It comes as no surprise that, within Amazon, outstanding employees are known as 'athletes', defined by such characteristics as 'endurance, speed and performance that can be measured, and an ability to defy limits'.[29]

Every year, Bezos writes a letter to shareholders, accompanied each time by a copy of his very first letter from 1997. In that first letter, Bezos stated that the three-year-old company, which had just achieved revenues of US$147.8 million (838 per cent growth compared to the previous year) and served more than 1.5 million customers, was still in its infancy – as was the entire Internet.

Bezos was right. By 2016, Amazon.com had made huge further strides: net sales amounted to US$135.9 billion, operating income was US$4.2 billion, and the number of customers exceeded 300 million across more than 100 countries. Beginning with books, Amazon had become one of the largest retailers in the world in almost all categories. The three main 'pillars' of its business are Prime[30] (more than 50 million users), Marketplace[31] (more than 2 million third-party sellers) and Amazon Web Services[32]

---

[28] J. Ho, 'Where Would Thwarted Power Woman Dong Mingzhu Lead China's Appliance Giant Gree?' *Forbes*, 1 December 2016.

[29] J. Kantor and D. Streitfeld, 'Inside Amazon: Wrestling Big Ideas in a Bruising Workplace', *New York Times*, 15 August 2015.

[30] Amazon Prime is a paid subscription service that gives customers access to free two-day shipping, streaming video/music and other benefits. Estimated number of users: more than 40 million people.

[31] Amazon Marketplace is an e-commerce platform that enables third-party sellers to sell new and used offerings on Amazon.com.

[32] Amazon Web Services (AWS) is a service offering on-demand cloud computing platforms, a leading company in cloud services.

(the largest contributor to the company's profits). In addition, Amazon develops tablets, e-readers, smart home appliances, video-streaming services, and even an intelligent personal assistant called Alexa. In 2015, Amazon Studios, which produces television shows and films using a crowdsourcing model, won a Golden Globe and a number of other awards. Since its inception, Amazon has demonstrated a 32,844 per cent total shareholder return (industry adjusted), and its market capitalization is now more than US$500 billion. However, Bezos, who continues to manage the company, insists that 'it is always Day 1 and Amazon is only at the beginning of its journey'.[33]

Jeff Bezos was born to a teenage mother and a father who left the home after just one year of marriage. He graduated from Princeton University with a diploma in electrical engineering and computer science, and quickly established a career on Wall Street. He read in a report that the amount of information passing through the Internet had increased by 2,300 per cent and immediately began to develop a business plan to ride this wave. The idea of an 'everything store' came to him at the very beginning, but Bezos considered it more practical to start with books.

Amazon sold its first book in 1995. In a pitch to investors, Bezos optimistically forecast that the company's sales in 2000 would be around US$114 million. He developed the motto 'Get Big Fast' and relentlessly drove the business forward. In 1997, Amazon went public, raising US$54 million (Bezos asked employees not to celebrate this). By 2000, Amazon's sales had risen to more than US$1.6 billion – 14 times bigger than Bezos's optimistic forecast just five years earlier.

In 1999, Bezos returned to the idea of an 'everything store', and Amazon began to sell products in other categories. He commented, 'We don't view ourselves as a bookstore or a music store. We want to be the place for someone to find and discover anything they want to buy.'[34] Later, he went even further and launched two new initiatives (or as some Amazon employees called them, 'fever dreams'): the Alexandria Project, aimed at obtaining

[33] Amazon's Letter to shareholders, 2016.
[34] B. Stone, *The Everything Store: Jeff Bezos and the Age of Amazon* (New York: Little, Brown and Company, 2013), p. 67.

two copies of every book ever printed, and the Fargo Project, aimed at obtaining one of every product ever manufactured and storing it in a distribution centre. Today, Amazon sells more than 368 million products, with electronics the biggest category.

From the very beginning, Amazon formulated its core mission as 'to raise the bar across the industries and around the world for what it means to be customer oriented'.[35] Instead of focusing on competitors, Bezos developed a 'customer-obsession' approach and never missed an opportunity to remind people of this in interviews or official statements. Anyone can send a letter to Bezos's email address (jeff@amazon.com); he reads them all and sometimes forwards complaints to the relevant managers with just one question mark as text. In addition, Bezos hates call centres, considering them proof of an inefficient customer experience. According to his philosophy, customers sometimes do not even know that they are unhappy: 'Customers are always beautifully, wonderfully dissatisfied, even when they report being happy and business is great.'[36]

Bezos is known to be extremely difficult to work for. He is very demanding, has zero tolerance for any kind of mistakes or mediocrity, and is prone to temper tantrums. Amazon's employees have even collected some 'Jeffisms', the phrases Bezos uses when he is angry, such as 'I'm sorry, did I take my stupid pills today?', 'Are you lazy or just incompetent?' and 'We need to apply some human intelligence to this problem' (after someone presented a proposal).[37] At the same time, employees all admit that this is not because he likes to drive people to tears. He just does not tolerate stupidity (or what appears to him as stupidity).

Despite his fiery temper, Bezos has the ability to stay calm in a crisis. As a result of the dot-com collapse in 2000, Amazon lost 90 per cent of its value. As he witnessed other companies going bankrupt, Bezos refused to mourn: 'Every minute spent thinking about the short-term stock price is a minute wasted.'[38] At the same

---

[35] Ibid. p. 10.
[36] Amazon's Letter to shareholders, 2016.
[37] B. Stone, *The Everything Store: Jeff Bezos and the Age of Amazon* (New York: Little, Brown and Company, 2013), p. 175.
[38] A. Jones, 'The Riff: Jeff Bezos and Long-Termism', *Financial Times*, 30 December 2015.

time, he was quite open with investors, admitting that 'we are not a stock you can sleep well with at night'.[39] As one of his colleagues later commented, 'I have never seen anyone so calm in the eye of a storm. Ice water runs through his veins.'[40]

After the 2000 dot-com collapse, Bezos quickly redefined Amazon. Instead of the 'Get Big Fast' motto, he adopted a new operating paradigm: 'Get Our House in Order' – with three key phrases: discipline, efficiency and eliminating waste. Some thought that Bezos would not be able to lift his foot off the accelerator and live in line with this new approach. As Scott Cook, an Amazon director at that time, said, 'Up until that point, I had seen Jeff only at one speed, the go-go speed of grow at all costs. I had not seen him drive toward profitability and efficiency. Most execs, particularly first-time CEOs who get good at one thing, can only dance what they know how to dance.'[41] Investors appreciated Bezos's efforts, and Amazon's shares returned to their pre-crisis level in 2003.

Achieving profitability required Bezos to understand retail even better, so he searched for knowledge wherever he could find it – from books (one of his favourites is *Made in America* by Sam Walton), competitors and executives. A former colleague remarked, 'Jeff was learning as he went along. He learned things from each of us who had expertise and incorporated the best pieces into his mental model. Now, everyone is expected to think as much as they can, like Jeff.'[42] Bezos's curiosity and his ability to learn quickly are widely known. He started an executive book club (on Saturday mornings so as not to distract people from work), invited prominent academics and scientists such as Jim Collins (author of *Good to Great*) and Clayton M. Christensen (author of *The Innovator's Dilemma*) to give lectures and tried to implement these ideas in real life.

The crucial factor in Bezos's success was not only making high-quality decisions but also making them quickly: 'Most decisions should probably be made with somewhere around 70% percent

[39] 'The Dotcom Wreckage', *The Economist*, 21 March 2001.
[40] Stone, *The Everything Store*, p. 103.
[41] Ibid., p. 104.
[42] Ibid., p. 332.

of the information you wish you had. If you wait for 90 percent, in most cases, you're probably being slow.'[43] In such fast-moving industries as technology and retail, 'if you invent a new way of doing something, typically if you are lucky, you get about two years of runway before competitors copy your idea. And two years is actually pretty long in a fast-moving industry.'[44]

Bezos insists that Amazon is not the fastest adopter but a true pathfinder: 'We have a pioneering culture – there are other very effective business strategies, pioneering is not the most effective one. Close following can be a very good business strategy, but it is just not who we are.'[45]

The best description of Amazon's culture is perhaps Bezos's widely cited motto: 'You can work hard, you can work long, you can work smart, but at Amazon you can't choose two of three.' In August 2015, the *New York Times* published an article entitled 'Inside Amazon: Wrestling Big Ideas in a Bruising Workplace',[46] and it had a bombshell effect. The authors called Amazon's corporate culture 'purposeful Darwinism', with a performance curve system that kept people in perpetual fear of layoff, crying at their desks and with a lack of work-life balance. Bezos reacted immediately. In a memo to employees, he commented, 'I strongly believe that anyone working in a company that really is like the one described in the New York Times would be crazy to stay.'[47] The *New York Times* indeed speculated that there is a high turnover of employees compared to other technology companies, but Amazon denies this. Over the years, there have been several cases of mass management exodus, but Bezos has always minimized their importance, as he strongly believes that no one is indispensable (excluding perhaps the CEO).

Some companies try to copy Amazon. For example, Uber proudly states that it has built an 'Amazonian' corporate culture.[48] But this is not the typical culture of a technology company.

---

[43] Amazon's Letter to shareholders, 2016
[44] C. Rose, 'Interview with Jeff Bezos', *Charlie Rose.com*, 27 October 2016.
[45] Ibid.
[46] Kantor and Streitfeld, 'Inside Amazon'.
[47] Jeff Bezos's memo to Amazon employees, 17 August 2015.
[48] R. Waters, 'Amazon's Jeff Bezos Pushes Speed and Intuition', *The Financial Times*, 13 April 2017.

Employees do not enjoy lavish perks, such as free parking, business-class travel or free meals. Frugality is one of Amazon's 14 'Leadership Principles'.[49]

As one of the pioneers of online retail, Amazon has faced the close scrutiny of government. For many years, it fought with several US states over Internet sales tax. Online retailers were not required to collect sales taxes on items sold in states where they did not have a physical presence. When, for example, Texas and Illinois tried to collect back taxes from the company, Amazon threatened to pull out of the state. However, in 2013, Amazon backed a bill in Congress to require online retailers to collect sales taxes in *all* states, explaining that a single system was preferable to a patchwork of rules. Another reason might be that Amazon had already moved to a one-day shipping policy, which would require a physical presence in all states. The issue still remains one of Bezos's major headaches: 'It's even a bipartisan issue that both sides agree on and we still can't get it done. It's very puzzling to me as an outsider, I don't know how you guys live here, honestly.'[50]

Growth has forced Amazon to become more attentive to government. In 2014, Bezos hired a former White House press secretary. He also bought the *Washington Post* for US$250 million and immediately used the newspaper as a lobbying tool. In 2016, Amazon doubled its lobbying expenditures to around US$9.4 million per year. Issues varied from taxes to regulation of drone fleets, immigration policies, cybersecurity and provision of cloud services to government agencies.

The US presidential campaign of 2016 represented a major challenge for Bezos. Donald Trump, presumably frustrated with the *Washington Post*'s investigation into his business empire, tweeted, 'The Washington Post, which loses a fortune, is owned by Jeff Bezos for purposes of keeping taxes down at his no-profit company, Amazon.'[51] He later expanded, 'I have respect for Jeff

---

[49] The other 13 are Customer Obsession; Ownership; Invent and Simplify; Are Right, A Lot; Learn and Be Curious; Hire and Develop the Best; Insist on the Highest Standards; Think Big; Bias for Action; Earn Trust; Dive Deep; Have Backbone: Disagree and Commit; Deliver Results.

[50] A. Peterson, 'Why Amazon Is Doubling Down on Lobbying', *Washington Post*, 5 February 2016.

[51] Donald Trump, Official Twitter account, @realDonaldTrump.

Bezos, but he uses the Washington Post to have political influence and I got to tell you, we have a different country than we used to have. He owns Amazon, he wants political influence so that Amazon will benefit from it. That's not right. And believe me, if I become president, oh do they have problems, they are going to have such problems.'[52] Bezos struck back, promising to reserve a seat for Trump on his Blue Origin rocket and send him into space. Speaking at a conference, Bezos also claimed that Trump's behaviour 'erodes our democracy around the edges'.[53]

However, immediately after Trump's victory, Bezos congratulated him on Twitter: 'Congratulations to @realDonaldTrump. I for one give him my most open mind and wish him great success in his service to the country.'[54] Trying to bury the hatchet during a meeting between the newly elected president and tech executives, Bezos introduced himself as 'Jeff Bezos, Amazon.com. Super excited about the possibility this could be the innovation administration'[55], while other executives just gave their names and the companies they represented.

Conversations about a possible successor to Bezos began as early as 1999, when the board of directors convinced him to hire Joe Galli from Black & Decker as COO, with the prospect of him replacing Bezos (then aged 35) some time in the future. This did not work out. To remedy the situation, the board consulted a coach, Bill Campbell, who, after interviewing both the CEO and the COO, recommended firing Galli: 'Why would you ever replace him [Bezos]? He's out of his mind, so brilliant at what he does.'[56] In December 2014, Bezos mentioned that Amazon's succession plan existed, but as of 2017 it remained a secret.

The third-wealthiest person in the world (according to *Forbes*), Bezos seems to have limitless energy. Together with Bill Gates, he has invested in a company that aims to detect cancer in its

---

[52] G. Ruddick, 'Amazon v Donald Trump? Jeff Bezos May Soon Face His Biggest Challenge Yet', *The Guardian*, 18 November 2016.

[53] Jeff Bezos Interview, *Vanity Fair's New Establishment Summit*, October 2016.

[54] Jeff Bezos, Official Twitter account, @jeffbezos.

[55] E. Kim, 'Here's How Amazon CEO Jeff Bezos Introduced Himself to Trump, after Months of Animosity', *Business Insider*, 14 December 2016.

[56] M. Moe, 'Tech Startup Secrets of Bill Campbell, Coach of Silicon Valley', *Forbes*, 27 July 2011.

earliest stages. But his main passion is space ('You don't choose your passions, your passions choose you'[57]). In 2000, he founded Blue Origin with the mission of lowering the cost of space travel and building infrastructure that will enable future generations to move all heavy industry into space. He remarked, 'If I'm 80 years old, looking back on my life and the one thing I have done is make it so that there is this gigantic entrepreneurial explosion in space for the next generation, I will be a happy man.'[58]

Other athletic leaders may have their grand designs, but Bezos's ambitions are, it seems, literally out of this world.

[57] Rose, Interview with Jeff Bezos.
[58] Ibid.

9

Athletic Leadership for Non-Athletes

I start early, and I stay late, day after day after day.
— Lionel Messi

Don't let anybody work harder than you do.
— Serena Williams

You only stop learning when you quit playing.
— Ruud Gullit

Athletic leadership is not a universal model of business leadership. It is highly contextual and situational. The athletic CEOs described in this book operate in turbulent contexts with a high level of government intervention and vertical leadership tradition. They started with a relatively low base – their companies lagged behind competitions or did not exist at all in the industries with lucrative domestic and international markets. However, its implications go beyond superambitious, curious, highly energetic chief executives operating in rapidly changing, turbulent environments with high levels of government participation. We believe that 'non-athletic' CEOs, aspiring leaders, politicians and most of us living in today's world can learn a lesson from the protagonists of this book and borrow some of their practices. In this concluding chapter we present key insights for each category of readers and outline some avenues for future research.

Lessons for Business Leaders

The practice of athletic leadership on a daily basis is a challenging and highly demanding task. It may not suit everybody's tastes or abilities. However, other leaders can benefit from it by using the following approaches.

Borrowing Some Elements and Instruments of Athletic Leadership to Complement Current Leadership Practice

While working on this research project we presented the model of athletic leadership at a workshop for CEOs. Our participants recognized a pattern that they had previously seen in some of their colleagues but generally dismissed athletic leadership as aggressive and egoistic. None of the seven attendees wanted to be an athletic leader. A few months later, three of them told us that they had started using some of the tools we discussed, specifically the metapractice of 'slack rope'; the setting of a leadership agenda with financial and transformational goals; and the practice of 'going out, going down, and going deep'. The CEOs had found these experiences positive, even though they had not turned into fans of athletic leadership.

We have repeated throughout this book that business leadership is highly situational: it is up to business leaders themselves to choose the elements of athletic leadership that will work in their contexts. However, we believe that two of the metapractices we have described – pragmatic exploration and navigating towards a moving target – are very relevant to the work of most of today's business leaders.

The first of these two metapractices represents a systemic approach to dealing with the challenge of rapid obsolescence of knowledge in all its forms – from human skills and mental models to products and technologies. This challenge will only intensify with time, and every business leader will have to find his or her own solution to it. Pragmatic exploration (see page 47) offers a tried and tested blueprint. It allows a leader to learn on a continuous basis, to make followers learn, to create and to sustain a knowledge-based learning organization. As Jeff Immelt, CEO of GE, once told us in an interview, 'You become a CEO not because of what you know but because of how fast you can learn, and that's something that people don't always understand. There is a projection of what the world will be like in 5, 10, 15 or 20 years, and can a person continue to meet that change as time goes on?'[1]

The second metapractice, navigating towards a moving target (see page 51), allows executives to fulfil the traditional leadership function of setting direction and reducing uncertainty in turbulent environments. Recently we have witnessed how turbulence is becoming a permanent feature of the global landscape, not just of some industries or regions. Brexit, the election of Donald Trump and his first steps as president show that even the most apparently stable and predictable institutions can be unexpectedly and quickly disrupted. Increasing turbulence makes the need for clear goals even more important, and navigating towards a moving target is the approach many business leaders can use to satisfy this need of their employees.

Using Athletic Leadership for a Specific Project or Task

This is another way of benefiting from the ideas in this book. Virtually every business leader in the world faces tasks or situations which to some degree resemble the context of our athletic leaders – fluid, turbulent, uncertain and with the active participation of powerful stakeholders. These call for an injection of athletic leadership. Executives who do not have the necessary ingredients, such as toughness and adaptability, or who do not subscribe to this method of working with their followers, can use it for a limited period of time and for a specific project. One of the participants of the CEOs' workshop shared his story:

> I am not a big fan of the people you studied, although I appreciate their achievements. From my business school years I believe in distributed leadership and see my role as creating conditions for the independent work of other people. As a CEO I don't need to bombard them with new ideas every day, challenge their performance, intervene with their team and, least of all, force them to work out in the gym. But I have to admit, recently I used what may have looked like your athletic leadership. We

[1] In interview with authors.

are working on an important investment project, which will cost more than half a billion dollars. It's the first time our company has undertaken such an ambitious project, and at this stage we are working on selecting a main contractor. I had one of the VPs managing this project, and at some point I realized that we were not getting anywhere because nobody, including the project leader, had done it before. Our people lacked the knowledge and courage to admit it. I rolled up my sleeves and dove into this project. Like an athletic leader, I started to learn details and had my people learn with me. I reset the goals a few times, manually steered key employees and took over as a chief negotiator. For three months I worked in this unnatural way for me, but we signed a contract.[2]

When a leader needs to undertake an organizational transformation project, make the company leapfrog the competition, withstand an unexpected crisis or enter a new line of business or a new region, athletic leadership can be the most appropriate model.

Aspiring Business Leaders

We work a great deal with young people who have decided to dedicate themselves to creating and managing business enterprises. We admire them for their courage, but we do not envy them. The complexity and turbulence of the world in which they will have to operate is daunting – if not terrifying. We will not tire our readers by listing the global trends that will shape business in the next decades, because nobody knows today what will or will not have an impact. But we all realize that the world will be more complex and will create new challenges for people who dare to take on leadership roles.

Can the athletic leadership model and the stories of this book's protagonists help future leaders prepare? We believe that they offer some interesting lessons to the next generation.

The major lesson is that effective leadership cannot be 'downloaded', no matter how advanced the user is. People become good leaders by practicing leadership, working hard, making bold moves and bouncing back from failures. Young people have a huge advantage. They can not only cherry-pick some specific

[2] In interview with authors.

practices of athletic leaders but also shape their own attitudes and cognitive abilities as well as develop tailor-made leadership habits.

Some elements of athletic leadership look especially important for today's future leaders, who themselves are – or will work with – millennials and representatives of Generation Z. Sociologists and psychologists tell us that these people strive for comfort, have hedonistic tendencies, jump from one activity to another and may easily back away from challenging tasks. Leaders will have to overcome such tendencies in themselves and compensate for these attitudes among their followers. Three elements of the athletic leadership mindset will be critical: *ambition, focus, and athletic effort.*

Ambition nurtures leadership. As we have seen throughout this book, it makes people do extraordinary things with their organizations, their followers and themselves. Although we all have different inborn levels of ambition, simple habits borrowed from 'athletic' CEOs and top-level athletes can help aspiring leaders learn how to *practice ambition.* Some of these are

- choosing the best in class for benchmarking;
- planning to beat your own record;
- following high-achieving role models from business and other areas; and
- 'slicing' ambition into achievable weekly, monthly and annual goals.

Maintaining concentration is becoming more and more challenging in today's world, which constantly bombards us with stimuli and distractions in the form of emails, messages, social networks, phone calls, advertising and more. Yet winning requires *focus.* Athletic leaders have proved it and demonstrated how focus can be another practical leadership habit in the world of shortening attention spans, multitasking and job-hopping.

Winning also requires *hard work.* This simple habit of athletic CEOs becomes critically important in a world of hedonism, artificial intelligence and multiple devices designed to make human lives easier. The ability to work long hours, under time pressure, in uncertain (and often hostile) environments, withstanding direct and indirect attacks, recovering from failures and deriving satisfaction from winning big rather than enjoying every minute of life, will serve the next generation of leaders as well as it has served the protagonists of this book. Aspiring leaders will also benefit from the habit of learning from failure, quickly bouncing back from adversity and looking at constraints as opportunities and enablers rather than threats.

We believe that a dose of toughness will be essential for effective leadership in the years to come. The earlier future leaders start training to be tough, the greater their chances of making it part of their mental and behavioural routines.

Toughness may or may not be a core trait of effective business leaders 20 years from now, but the importance of *mental adaptability* cannot be overestimated. Increasing complexity, combined with the speed and scale of change in the business environment, requires a flexible, adaptable and innovative leadership mindset. We are certain that aspiring leaders will greatly improve their chances of success by emulating athletic leaders in this respect: actively seeking new data, knowledge and experience from multiple sources; unlearning outdated concepts and habits; and adjusting their mental models. The metapractice of pragmatic exploration should become one of their fundamental leadership routines.

Learning toughness and adaptability from athletic leaders will not guarantee today's youngsters an easy ride on their way to the top, but it will create a solid foundation for their leadership experiments. Their goals, tools, outputs and outcomes will be defined by the contexts in which they operate, as much as by themselves. From this perspective, mastering more specific practices of athletic leaders – such as *Making clothes with room for growth* or *Going out, going deep and going down* – may be of less importance. However, these and others could be good starting points, especially under the conditions of high uncertainty that many inexperienced leaders face.

We would like to conclude this section by emphasizing the major risk for aspiring leaders interested in learning from athletic CEOs – copying! Athletic leaders are effective precisely because they understand their environments and constraints and operate within these limits. They *never* borrow ideas or instruments without adjusting them, blindly transferring what they do into other contexts, because they know it will result in failure. Athletic leadership is a model that not only allows for but also *requires* intelligent application.

Politicians

As this book is being written, the world of politics is going through a deep crisis both in developed and developing, democratic and not-so-democratic countries. Traditional politics and political elites have failed to find adequate solutions to the challenges of a rapidly evolving world: ending wars and preventing new ones; effectively containing terrorism; reducing international tensions; protecting the environment; and eradicating poverty and diseases. Alternative politicians, such as Donald Trump in the United States and Rodrigo Duterte in the Philippines, or the (as yet) unelected Marine Le Pen in France or Geert Wilders in the Netherlands offer a return to the past as the solution. Although this 'new wave' may bear some resemblance to our athletic CEOs in terms of their high energy, tough talk and competitiveness, the similarity is only surface deep. On the contrary, we believe that athletic leaders offer a very different approach, from which both 'traditional' and 'new wave' politicians could learn a few lessons.

Transformational Ambition

Like athletic CEOs, contemporary politicians are superambitious people who let nothing stand in their way. However, their ambitions are almost always personal and linked to staying in power. Athletic CEOs also care about keeping their jobs but only as a means to an end. Their real ambition is to bring about change that can be measured and appreciated by others. The world needs politicians who are passionate about positive change, not just winning another election. To develop more productive ambitions, politicians should consider borrowing the metapractice of pragmatic exploration from athletic CEOs.

Pragmatic Exploration

Pragmatic exploration takes athletic CEOs away from their corner offices and puts them in touch with reality – people from all walks of life, organizations, ideas, management practices, products and technologies. It allows them to stay in touch with a complex world on a continuous basis so that they can formulate and reformulate their visions as well as their strategies for mobilizing people to achieve them. This is exactly what today's politicians need: to get out of their offices, to dig down and deep, to collect data and work with it, to experiment on a small scale and learn from it, to drop projects that are outdated and initiate new ones. They should replace their practice of 'going to the people' once every electoral cycle with a process of ongoing exploration.

For politicians who are given a mandate for change, athletic leadership offers a blueprint for the turnaround programme. Elected or appointed politicians who aspire to transform need to formulate a leadership agenda with specific short- and long-term goals – both outputs and outcomes, metrics and projects. They need to try it out and adjust it as required. They can choose all or some of the metapractices in the athletic CEOs' toolbox. Or they may even consider asking one of them to be a mentor!

As we were preparing this book for publication Emmanuel Macron, recently elected French President, began to demonstrate how some elements of Athletic Leadership could work in a political context. Not only he set very ambitious goals for the country, the European Union, his government and for each of his ministers to be achieved within a short period of time (some of them such as labor code and wealth tax reforms have already been realized), but started to apply such tools of Athletic Leaders as *Navigating towards a moving target*, *Pragmatic Exploration*, *Slack Rope* and *Quiet Recognition*. The new President works very hard, learns very fast and makes sure other members of his team do the same.[3]

General Public

The authors of this book do not consider themselves business leaders. Nor do we aspire to business leadership. But we have learned a few tricks from our athletic CEOs and would like to share some insights that may be relevant to people from all occupations and ways of life.

[3] Nouzille, V. 'Les Hommes du President', *Le Figaro Magazine*, November 17, 2017

Goal setting is a universal human activity. And psychologists keep reminding us that healthy doses of competition and assertiveness are essential for human development and well-being. Athletic leadership teaches us to be more ambitious, more competitive and to aim higher. We should all strive for personal bests, high performance and big wins. Yet, at the same time, we should not pursue goals that have lost their relevance. Instead, we should adjust them to changing conditions and circumstances. Above all, we should not regret unfulfilled ambitions or dramatize unrealized plans.

Athletic leaders give us a lesson in self-confidence, but theirs is not an empty confidence. They believe in their ability to win, because they know they have done their homework. And they have been doing it for decades. Properly substantiated confidence could make the lives of many people more enjoyable and fulfilling.

Exploration is another practice we can all borrow from athletic CEOs. For many professionals this is an essential element of their work, which keeps them competitive. But the discovery of new things and the disposal of old baggage simply make human lives richer. People are programmed to explore and derive satisfaction from journeys into the unknown. These adventures may not always be pleasant, but we can learn from athletic leaders to be tough, stiffen our resolve and reap the benefits. The protagonists of this book demonstrate that resilience is a practice that can be learned.

Athletic leaders are also masters of building, maintaining and extracting value from social ties. They value relationships, nurture them and invest time and other resources in them. Athletic CEOs are not transactional in their relationships with others, but they do not run social charities either. To be part of an athletic leader's network is to represent some potential value (resources, ideas, connections, emotions etc.) This careful approach to managing professional networks could be beneficial to all of us.

Leadership Development Professionals

Just as athletic CEOs are passionate about building world-class companies, so too are we passionate about developing world-class leaders. In our experience, the contribution of good teachers, coaches, mentors and advisers to the development and performance of business leaders cannot be overstated. We have derived a number of valuable insights from studying athletic leaders and have already begun to use these in our leadership development practice. We would like to share them with other leadership development professionals.

Attention to All Aspects That Define Leadership

Our study shows that a leader's past, mindset and way of thinking as well as specific characteristics of the near and wider environments have a defining impact on his or her goals and practices. This finding has two consequences for people whose job it is to help leaders become more effective. First, there is a need to direct attention to these factors, to assist leaders in understanding them and to help identify their influence. This awareness building can take various formats, from coaching sessions to questionnaires, and should enlighten leaders about themselves and their contexts. Second, there is a need to help leaders work on their psychological and cognitive capabilities. These can be improved – even later in life – and can become important sources of additional effectiveness.

Defining the Leadership Agenda

A leadership agenda is a powerful tool for achieving desired outputs, outcomes and learning. In our work with business leaders we help them master this instrument by going through a number of steps. First, they clarify their ambition. Second, they plot their leadership journey over a period of time. Third, they break it into outputs and outcomes for each year (or number of months) within this period of time. Fourth, they assign a metric to each desired output and outcome, whether a quantitative indicator or a qualitative way to measure progress. Fifth, they define a limited number of key projects to achieve each output and outcome. Finally, they determine a procedure to review progress and make adjustments.

Leadership Practices

We have found the construct of a 'leadership practice' – a specific, iterative, action-oriented behaviour strategy – to be very useful in helping executives understand and improve their performance. It allows leaders to picture their work as the continuous application of a limited number of practices (usually there are from 5 to 15 core practices), to analyse how productive each of them is (including costs versus benefits), and to adjust their 'portfolio' by eliminating some practices, strengthening others and adding new ones. This tool makes leadership benchmarking easier to conduct and reflect on. We have found that leaders are more receptive to learning a new practice than to developing a competency or skill.

Our work with leadership practices has reinforced another lesson from athletic CEOs – *the need to unlearn and eliminate* outdated behavioural and mental practices. We have observed that many of our clients subconsciously continue doing something just because it has worked in the past. This practice no longer adds value but rather takes time, energy and organizational resources, and creates a feeling of doing something important. Coaches and advisers should help leaders recognize and get rid of such practices. As Peter Drucker taught us many decades ago, such periodical reinvigoration of an executive's repertoire is a must during the times of rapid change. Unless we can liberate our space, mind and soul from the baggage of the past, rapid development is impossible.

Scholars of Leadership

This book is not an academic monograph. Our goal was to present the model of athletic leadership to a wider audience, including practicing and future leaders in business and other fields, their followers, coaches, educators and the general public. Yet we believe that our research has opened up a number of avenues to be noted and possibly followed by scholars of leadership.

Most leadership literature concentrates on 'effective', 'productive' or 'ideal' models of leadership (such as emotional intelligence or adaptive leadership), or distinguishes between 'good' and 'bad' leadership (for example, transformational versus transactional, or democratic versus coercive). The model of athletic leadership follows a different approach. It is based on and describes 'real' leadership – living, breathing CEOs with strengths and shortcomings, operating in a specific environment and producing 'positive' and 'negative' results. We believe that this model is a richer representation of leadership reality and that a more phenomenological approach will bring valuable future insights into the study of leadership in business.

The existing scholarly models of leadership often identify and describe a single element that defines a leader's effectiveness – power, emotional intelligence achievement motivation, organizational constraints and so on. With athletic leadership, we offer a complex multivariable model.

We have identified two basic traits, *toughness and adaptability*, which are often seen as mutually exclusive, but that in the case of athletic leaders coexist dynamically and define their leadership. Toughness makes them competitive, proactive, focused and tolerant of temporary inconvenience. Adaptability allows them to develop, constantly expand and update their mental models, and to get rid of obsolete assumptions and habits.

We have also described *two situational elements* of athletic leadership: leadership agendas and leadership practices. Leadership scholars and leadership development specialists still concentrate too much on personality traits or leadership competencies. We believe that shifting the focus from fixed to more flexible elements of leadership would allow leadership theory to advance and improve the effectiveness of leadership development efforts.

We have made *leadership practices* – iterative behaviour strategies – the core of our research into athletic leadership. We share the view of activity theorists that people not only express but also create themselves in action. Most importantly, we believe that description of practices provides insights into the essence of athletic leadership and allows other people to learn and enhance their effectiveness. In this book we have presented a comprehensive list of metapractices of athletic leaders.

We have conceptualized that application of leadership agendas and leadership practices creates two different types of results: *leadership outputs and outcomes*. The first term describes current operational and financial results of the companies the leaders run, while the second refers to their impact on followers, organizations and communities. Such distinctions emphasize that leadership is not simply a business function but also a transformative social relationship.

We believe that the multilevel, multivariable contingency model presented in this book can be used in studying other leadership phenomena in different contexts.

In our opinion, the phenomenon of athletic leadership itself deserves further scholarly exploration. In this book we have presented athletic leadership as a situational, context-specific model of effective leaders and illustrated it with examples from Russia, and also some other countries, mainly emerging economies. The model itself would benefit from further refining, using examples from other contexts, especially the less developed economies of Africa, Asia and Latin America, as well as mature, successful and complex companies operating across borders.

It would also be interesting to apply a psychodynamic lens to athletic leadership in order to deepen our understanding of such aspects as the leader's personality; his or her motivation and drive at both conscious and subconscious levels; and leader-team and leader-organization dynamics. A detailed study of corporate cultures at 'athletically led companies', including their artefacts, espoused values, basic assumptions and collective psychological defence mechanisms would shed further new light on the outcomes of athletic leadership.

We have studied athletic leaders as they started their CEO jobs and mastered them. It will be very interesting to see if and how their leadership will evolve as they enter their second decade in the role. A longitudinal study of the protagonists of this book and other athletic leaders would provide insights into the very interesting question of how flexible and sustainable athletic leadership is. Such research could trace changes over time in both independent and dependent variables and their interrelation. Our hypothesis is that athletic CEOs will continue to expand their playing field. For example, Jeff Bezos just added Whole Foods to his portfolio. We believe that the increasing complexity of business will be the main challenge to the CEO-centred model of athletic companies, and we would not like to bet on how effectively they will deal with it. Whether athletic leaders will be effective in leading representatives of Generation Z is another question worth exploring. Gref for one has acknowledged it as a more pressing challenge than working with the government.

Another challenge awaiting all athletic leaders is succession. We have not had a chance to observe an athletic CEO transferring his or her power, so we can only hypothesize at this stage. We feel that athletic leaders will concentrate on leading rather than preparing their successors and will 'run (their businesses) till they drop' (or get dropped). Their supersized ambition and competitiveness make them unlikely candidates for effective management of personal succession – the boards of their companies will probably have to take care of this task. We also feel that the boards should look externally because athletic CEOs leave too little room for new leaders to develop. Boards may even think about replacing an athletic leader with two or more compatible executives who will complement each other and will collectively ensure an adequate level of mental toughness and adaptability at the top.

Researching and writing this book was an exciting and enlightening journey. We have discovered a whole new universe of athletic leaders – passionate, ambitious people who take on enormous challenges and produce remarkable results by being determined and focused, constantly learning and making thousands of other people dream big, aim high, develop and perform. This journey has also changed us, and we are grateful to the protagonists of this book for giving us this opportunity.

Further Reading

Adair, J. E. *Leadership for Innovation: How to Organise Team Creativity and Harvest Ideas*. London and Philadelphia: Kogan Page, 2007.

Bennis, W., and Spreitzer G. M. *The Future of Leadership: Today's Top Leadership Thinkers Speak to Tomorrow's Leaders*. San Francisco: Jossey-Bass, 2001.

Charan, R. *Leaders at All Levels: Deepening Your Talent Pool to Solve the Succession Crisis*. San Francisco: John Wiley & Sons, 2008.

Coles, M. J., and Southworth, G. (eds). *Developing Leadership: Creating the Schools of Tomorrow*. New York: Open University Press, 2005.

Conger, J. A. *The Practice of Leadership: Developing the Next Generation of Leaders*. San Francisco: Jossey-Bass, 2007.

Donaldson, Gordon A. Jr. *Cultivating Leadership In Schools: Connecting People, Purpose, & Practice.* New York: Teachers College, Columbia University, 2006.

Giber, D., Lam, S., Goldsmith, M. and Bourke, J. (eds). *Linkage Inc.'s Best Practices in Leadership Development Handbook: Case Studies, Instruments, Training.* San Francisco: Pfeiffer, 2009.

Johansen, B. *Leaders Make the Future: Ten New Leadership Skills for an Uncertain World.* San Francisco: Berrett-Koehler Publishers, 2009.

Kets de Vries, M. F. R., Shekshnia, S., Korotov, K. and Florent-Treacy, E. *The New Russian Business Leaders: New Horizons in Leadership Studies.* Cheltenham: Edward Elgar, 2004.

Khurana, R., and Nohria, N. (eds). *Handbook of Leadership Theory and Practice.* Boston: Harvard Business School Press, 2010.

Knippenberg, van D., and Hogg M. A. *Leadership and Power: Identity Processes in Groups and Organizations.* Thousand Oaks, CA: SAGE Publications, 2003.

Maeda, J. *Redesigning Leadership: Design, Technology, Business, Life.* Cambridge, MA: MIT Press, 2011.

Marx, G. *Future-focused Leadership: Preparing Schools, Students, and Communities for Tomorrow's Realities.* Alexandria, VA: Association for Supervision and Curriculum Development, 2006.

Muna, F. A., and Zennie, Z. A. *Developing Multicultural Leaders: The Journey to Leadership Success.* New York: Palgrave Macmillan, 2010.

Pfeffer, J. *Managing with Power: Politics and Influence in Organizations.* Boston: Harvard Business School Press, 1992.

Podolny, J. M., Khurana, R. and Hill-Popper, M. 'Revisiting the Meaning of Leadership', *Research in Organizational Behavior* 26 (2005): 1–36.

Reeves, M., and Harnoss, J. 'An Agenda for the Future of Global Business', *Harvard Business Review,* 27 February 2017.

Rhodes, R. A. W., and Hart, P. (eds). *The Oxford Handbook of Political Leadership.* Oxford: Oxford University Press, 2014.

Velsor, E., McCauley, C. and Ruderman, M. (eds). *The Center for Creative Leadership Handbook of Leadership Development.* San Francisco: Jossey-Bass, 2010.

Films and Television Series

Jiro Dreams of Sushi. Documentary film directed by David Gelb. New York: Magnolia Pictures, 2011.

The Young Pope. Mini-TV series directed by Paolo Sorrentino. Roma: Wildside, 2016.

Appendix: Research Methodology

Originally this book was planned as a sequel to *The New Russian Business Leaders* (Kets de Vries, M. F. R., Shekshnia S., Korotov K. and Florent-Treacy E., 2004). We wanted to see how the Russian business leadership landscape had evolved during the ensuing decade.

Our first finding was that the country's business context had undergone tremendous changes. On the one hand the Russian economy had caught up with the rest of the world during the growth years of the early 2000s, and global trends – such as digitalization, knowledge obsolescence, turbulence, climate change, terrorism and others – had made a much stronger impact on the work of Russian business leaders than previously. On the other hand Russia as a country had become more assertive in international affairs, more nationalistic and more protectionist. The role – and the direct participation – of the government in regulating the economy had increased dramatically. The crisis of 2008–9 was a strong blow to the Russian economy and only reinforced the government's activism.

These discoveries sharpened the focus of our research: we decided to find out what kind of leadership produces superior results in this turbulent context with its heavy government participation. Specifically, we wanted to address the following research questions:

1. Which Russian companies achieved exceptional results during the turbulent period of 2009–16?

2. What was the role of the leaders (CEOs) of these companies in assuring this performance?
3. What personal and behavioural characteristics of the CEOs enabled this leadership?
4. What do the leaders of these companies have in common?

We also wanted to examine complex organizations with sustainable superior financial performance, which were leaders in their industries in Russia and competitive globally. We looked at the performance of the 160 largest Russian businesses from 2003 to 2013 and selected a list of eight CEOs: Herman Gref (Sberbank), Vitaly Saveliev (Aeroflot), Alexander Dyukov (Gazprom Neft), Eugene Kaspersky (Kaspersky Lab), Oleg Bagrin (NLMK), Sergey Frank (Sovcomflot), Oleg Tinkov (Tinkoff Bank) and Sergey Galitsky (Magnit). Since we wanted to apply a clinical methodology, we had to choose people who were willing to spend time with researchers and allow access to their companies.

Eventually, the first four CEOs in our list became the main focus of our research. At the same time, we enormously enriched our understanding through interviews, conversations and observations of the four other business people.

Methods

We believed that we could develop insights into the minds and work of our protagonists by understanding the context in which they operate, being as close as possible to them, observing them in action, talking to them about their leadership and interviewing their followers, superiors and counterparts. We opted for a qualitative method of study, using some additional quantitative data analysis to assess their environments and challenges, as well as the performance of their companies.

In-depth Interviews

Our main research method was in-depth, semi-structured interviews with the four CEOs: Herman Gref, Vitaly Saveliev, Alexander Dyukov and Eugene Kaspersky. We met with each of them five to ten times. We interviewed 20 to 50 current and former employees of each company from different levels of the hierarchy – direct reports to the CEO, middle managers and rank-and-file employees. We also spoke to customers, suppliers, regulators, competitors and board members of our protagonists' companies, conducting 10 to 20 such interviews per company.

Observation of Participants

We had the opportunity to observe leaders and their companies from within at numerous occasions, such as board and management meetings, customer visits, suppliers' conferences, town hall meetings and employee gatherings. We observed from the inside how the leaders interacted with their followers, how they made decisions and communicated them to the organization, how they energized their troops and how they handled success and failure.

Action Research

At different times we worked with three out of four of the companies in a professional capacity. We not only observed but also in some way took part in the transformation of the leaders and companies we studied. We assumed the roles of invited speakers, facilitators of strategic sessions and executive coaches.

Qualitative Media Analysis

In researching this book we reviewed over 300 books and journal and newspaper articles about the leaders and their companies, video interviews with the CEOs and conference presentations. We studied internal publications and other communications materials of all four companies.

Quantitative Data Analysis

Three out of the four organizations we researched are public companies. We studied their annual reports and other stakeholder communications to understand their financial and operational performance and compare them to the competition.

Secondary Sources

The main ideas presented in this book were developed through a clinical study of four Russian CEOs. We relied on published sources to put together compact descriptions of the personalities and working methods of three athletic leaders from other countries: Roger Agnelli, former CEO of Vale (Brazil); Dong Mingzhu, CEO of Gree Electric (China); and Jeff Bezos, CEO of Amazon.com (United States).

Index